D0116445

COOKING AT A GLANCE

PASTA

FOG CITY PRESS

Published by Fog City Press
814 Montgomery Street
San Francisco, CA 94133 USA

Copyright © 1994 Weldon Owen Pty Ltd

Chief Executive Officer John Owen

President Terry Newell

Art Director Kylie Mulquin

Editorial Manager Janine Flew

Production Manager Gilly Biven

Production Coordinator Kylie Lawson

Business Manager Emily Jahn

Vice President International Sales
Stuart Laurence

Project Managing Editor Tori Ritchie

Contributing Editor Jane Horn

Project Designer Patty Hill

Food Photographer Chris Shorten

Steps Photographer Kevin Candland

Food Stylists Susan Massey
and Vicki Roberts-Russell

Prop Stylist Laura Ferguson

All rights reserved.
Unauthorized reproduction,
in any manner, is prohibited.

A catalog record for this book is
available from the Library of Congress,
Washington, DC.

ISBN 1-892374-48-X

Manufactured by Kyodo Printing Co.
(S'pore) Pte Ltd
Printed in Singapore
A Weldon Owen Production

Cover Recipe: Classic Tomato Sauce, page 18,
with ravioli
Opposite Page: Pasta & Prawns in Asparagus
Sauce, page 56

4

CONTENTS

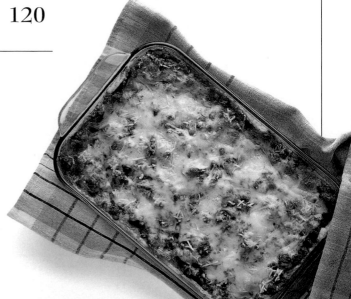

Introduction

PASTA: A SIMPLE ITALIAN WORD for a simple food that has appeared on Mediterranean and Asian tables since antiquity. Yet pasta has become so popular with cooks everywhere in recent years that it has also come to mean a world of good eating in almost any language.

Why has pasta been elevated from ethnic favorite to international culinary superstar? Probably because it fits in so well with today's cooking style. People want food that is light, easily prepared, and superbly fresh, made with the season's best offerings. Pasta's subtle flavor and slightly chewy texture make it a perfect partner for fresh vegetables and herbs. And not only is pasta good to eat and quick to serve up, it also provides a healthy bonus: High-carbohydrate, low-fat pasta fills an important role in a well-balanced diet.

If long, thin spaghetti or tubular elbow macaroni are the pasta shapes that you are most familiar with, you are about to embark on a delicious voyage of discovery. The editors of *Cooking at a Glance* have created sixty new recipes that showcase fresh and dried pasta in all its variety, including the wonderful packaged fresh pastas widely available in supermarkets today.

In the pages to come you will be introduced to little bow ties known as farfalle, to pleated radiatori, to circular ruote with spokes like wagon wheels, to tight little twists called fusilli, and to many more, including new and tempting interpretations of classics like tortellini, ravioli, and lasagne. You will also learn how easy it is to make plain, whole-wheat, spinach, tomato, and herb pasta in your own kitchen.

An introductory chapter covers the basics of preparing homemade pasta and the best way to cook your own or purchased pasta so that it is served properly al dente. Next is a collection of sauces infused with aromatic fresh herbs, pungent garlic, and garden-picked vegetables that you will use again and again. Succeeding chapters explore the pleasures of particular types of pasta: ribbon, shaped, and stuffed pastas; layered pasta dishes; and hot and cold pasta salads. Every chapter is color coded, and every recipe features a "steps-at-a-glance" box that uses these colors for quick reference to the photographic steps illustrating techniques used in the recipe. Tips appear throughout, from basic equipment needs to helpful hints to a glossary of ingredients. From first step to last, every recipe is guaranteed to please. Try elegant Stuffed Pasta Rolls the next time you entertain, or stir-fry a batch of Szechwan Chicken & Pasta for a quick after-work supper. Plan Sunday dinner around Spaghetti with Creamy Clam Sauce, an update of the popular seafood dish, or Baked Pasta & Cheddar with Ham, a sophisticated version of a childhood favorite. No matter which you choose, the result will be picture perfect, because it's all there for you, *at a glance.*

Stuffed Pasta Rolls, page 92

6

The Basics

Steps for Making Pasta

Making fresh pasta by hand requires mixing bowls and a wooden spoon plus a rolling pin to flatten the dough into paper-thin sheets and a knife to cut it into portions. To freeze the dough you will need a freezer-safe container.

ROLLING PIN

MIXING BOWLS

WOODEN SPOON

CHEF'S KNIFE

FREEZER-SAFE CONTAINER

8

MAKING PASTA BY HAND

MAKING PASTA is a little like culinary alchemy. With a minimum of mixing, kneading, and shaping, the simplest of ingredients — flour, water, oil, salt, and eggs — are transformed into edible gold. Homemade pasta is easy to prepare, whether by hand or with a simple pasta machine available at most cookware stores.

Why make your own pasta if you can purchase it ready made? You can taste the difference. The result is more tender and delicate than packaged pasta, and will more fully absorb whatever sauce coats it. However, a quality purchased fresh or dried pasta can be almost as good as the pasta you prepare from scratch.

On the pages to come you'll learn to make delicate narrow and wide ribbons, wrappers for stuffing mani-cotti and cannelloni, the little bundles known as ravioli and tortellini, and broad sheets for layered lasagne. You'll also discover the secrets to hand-shaping bow tie–shaped farfalle, the little cups called orecchiette, and more. For all of these and for any dish in the book that calls for homemade pasta, use the basic recipe on page 14. The recipe is so simple that after the first few times you prepare it you probably won't even need to refer to it, but for now you might want to put a marker on that page for quick reference. Or, use purchased fresh pasta, available in the refrigerated case of many supermarkets.

This section demonstrates the essential steps for making pasta dough completely by hand. The remainder of the chapter describes how to mix pasta dough with a food processor, and the proper way to knead and roll the dough with a hand-cranked pasta maker that clamps onto a kitchen counter or table. Succeeding chapters detail how to cut and shape pasta dough and how to identify and use the myriad dry pasta shapes available. Even the best pasta, whether fresh or dried, can be ruined if improperly cooked. The steps on pages 12 and 13 explain this elementary but critical technique. Throughout this book, recipes call for twice as much uncooked fresh pasta (homemade *or* purchased) as dried.

for herb pasta, add dried seasoning to flour mixture

for spinach pasta, add finely chopped cooked spinach to egg mixture

knead until dough is smooth and elastic (8 to 10 minutes)

STORING DOUGH

STEP 1 DIVIDING THE DOUGH

After kneading, shape the dough into a round; do not roll out. Divide the round into fourths or whatever portion size is specified in the recipe, using a sharp knife.

after cutting, shape each quarter portion into a ball and then flatten

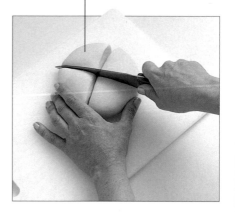

STEP 1 ADDING EGG MIXTURE TO FLOUR

Stir together flour and salt in a large mixing bowl. Make a well or depression in the center. In another bowl combine eggs, water, and oil and pour liquid into the well of the flour mixture. Mix thoroughly with a wooden spoon.

STEP 2 KNEADING BY HAND

Turn out the dough onto a lightly floured work surface. To knead, curve your fingers over the edge of the dough and pull it toward you. Then push down and away with the heel of your hand. Give the dough a quarter turn, fold toward you, and repeat the process. Cover and let rest for 10 minutes before rolling out.

9

if the dough shrinks back while rolling, let it rest several minutes under a kitchen towel or sheet of plastic wrap, then continue

the surface of rolled-out dough must dry somewhat or it will stick together when cut

STEP 2 FREEZING DOUGH

Wrap each portion airtight in plastic wrap. Then store in a freezer-safe container or in heavy-duty freezer bags. The dough will keep in the freezer for up to 8 months.

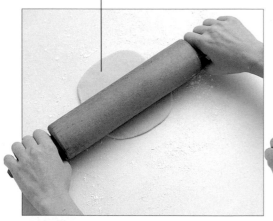

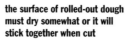

to use, thaw several hours in the refrigerator or about 1 hour at room temperature

STEP 3 ROLLING THE DOUGH

Divide the dough into recipe-sized portions, usually in fourths. Set one portion on a floured work surface. Flatten with a rolling pin to about a ⅛-inch thickness. Cover the remaining dough with a kitchen towel or plastic wrap so it won't dry out, or freeze for later use as shown at right.

STEP 4 ROLLING DOUGH TO ¹⁄₁₆ INCH

Continue rolling the dough until it is ¹⁄₁₆ inch thick. A one-quarter portion will roll out to a square that is about 12x12 inches. After rolling, let the dough rest, uncovered, for 20 minutes so the surface will dry slightly.

Steps for Making Pasta

BASIC TOOLS FOR MAKING PASTA BY MACHINE

To prepare pasta by machine, use a small bowl, a measuring cup, a rubber spatula, and a food processor to mix the ingredients, and a hand-cranked pasta maker to knead and roll the dough.

FOOD PROCESSOR

PASTA MACHINE

LIQUID CUP MEASURE

SMALL BOWL

RUBBER SPATULA

10

MAKING PASTA BY MACHINE

WHEN PASTA DOUGH is mixed in a food processor, then rolled to paper thinness in a manual pasta maker, the whole process becomes almost effortless.

As usual, the food processor does its job quickly. Monitor the dough at every step. If you don't have a pasta machine, you can knead food processor dough with your hands and roll it out with a rolling pin as shown in steps 2, 3, and 4 on the previous page. However, the hand-cranked pasta machine is relatively inexpensive compared to most home appliances and small enough to store out of sight when not in use. If you make pasta often, it might be a sensible purchase because it takes almost all of the work out of kneading and rolling.

Start at the lowest setting, with the rollers wide apart; usually two passes through each setting will be enough. If the sheet of dough feeds through the rollers easily and looks smooth and silky, almost rubbery, without rough spots, turn to the next setting. If you really have to crank hard, go back to a wider setting. Continue until the dough is the proper texture and thickness, usually 1/16 inch thick.

add chopped cooked spinach during this step if making spinach pasta by machine

STEP 1 PROCESSING DRY INGREDIENTS
Place flour, salt, and eggs in the work bowl of a food processor. Cover and process with a pulsing action until the mixture is the consistency of cornmeal. This happens very quickly, so don't overprocess.

stir the liquid ingredients with a fork before pouring so they will blend more smoothly

STEP 2 ADDING LIQUID

Put water, oil, and any other liquid in a measuring cup with a lip. With the processor running, slowly pour the liquid through the feed tube into the work bowl. The flour mixture will begin to form a cohesive mass.

if you let the dough rest after processing it will be easier to roll out

STEP 3 FORMING A BALL

Continue processing the mixture just until the dough forms a ball. Stop once or twice to scrape down the sides of the work bowl so all the ingredients are incorporated into the dough. Remove from the work bowl, cover, and let rest 10 minutes.

11

sprinkle dough lightly with flour before each pass through the machine so it doesn't stick

STEP 4 KNEADING IN PASTA MACHINE

Divide the dough into 4 portions or as directed in the recipe. Cover unused dough or freeze (see page 9). Flatten one portion and feed through the rollers at the widest setting. Fold in half or thirds, give a quarter turn, and run through the same setting. Repeat until the dough is smooth and no longer tears.

when done, let dough sheet rest for 20 minutes on a lightly floured towel before shaping

if dough becomes too long to handle, cut it in half

STEP 5 ROLLING IN PASTA MACHINE

Turn to the next narrower setting. Lightly flour the dough, fold, give a quarter turn, and pass through the machine again. Repeat folding, turning, and rolling at increasingly higher (narrower) settings until the dough is 1/16 inch thick.

Steps for Making Pasta

BASIC TOOLS FOR COOKING PASTA

A large pasta pot lets pasta tumble freely in the bubbling water. The cooking liquid drains away afterwards through a strainer insert or free-standing colander. Use a pasta rake for tossing and serving long strands.

COLANDER

WOODEN PASTA RAKE

PLASTIC PASTA RAKE

PASTA POT

12

COOKING PASTA

ALWAYS USE a large pot so pasta can circulate freely in vigorously boiling water with room to expand as it cooks. If the pot is too small the pasta will stick together; you also risk an overflow of the scalding, bubbling liquid. A pasta pot with a strainer insert is practical: It is the right size and lets you drain off the water with very little effort because the water flows back into the pot when you lift the insert. Salt may be added to the water for flavor and oil helps keep pasta from sticking, but neither is a must.

Fresh pasta never needs more than a few minutes to cook. Dried ribbons and shapes take longer, anywhere from 8 to 15 minutes (check the package for recommended cooking times). Both types are done when the texture is tender but still slightly chewy and no traces of raw pasta remain when you bite into a piece — a quality described as "al dente." Drain, then transfer to a warm serving bowl and toss immediately with sauce or use as directed in the recipe. A pasta rake in wood, metal, or plastic works best for tossing and serving pasta strands.

for long strands, like spaghetti, dip one end of the batch in water until softened, then curl it around pan and lower it into the water

STEP 1 ADDING PASTA TO WATER

Fill a large pot with 3 quarts of water (for 4 to 8 ounces of pasta). Bring to a vigorous, rolling boil. Add 1 teaspoon of salt and 1 tablespoon of oil, if desired. Then add the pasta, a little at a time, so the water stays at a boil.

adjust the heat, if
necessary, to keep
the water boiling

the Italians say pasta is
done when it is *al dente,*
or "to the tooth"

STEP 2 STIRRING OCCASIONALLY

Stir occasionally with a wooden spoon or pasta rake to keep the strands or pieces from sticking together as they swirl around in the water.

STEP 3 TESTING FOR DONENESS

Near the end of cooking time, taste often to check for doneness. Pasta is ready when the texture is tender, but still slightly firm, or "al dente." Don't let the pasta sit in the cooking water or it will overcook and get mushy.

For best flavor and texture, drain
pasta thoroughly so no cooking
water sticks to the pieces
and dilutes the sauce.

TIP BOX

TWO WAYS TO DRAIN

STEP 1 REMOVING DRAINER INSERT

If using a pasta pot with an insert, lift up the insert by the handles (protect your hands with hotpads, if necessary). The cooking water will drain back into the pot.

give the insert a few
shakes to remove any
remaining water from
the pasta

STEP 2 DRAINING IN A COLANDER

Set a colander in the sink. If using a standard pot without a drainer insert, pour the pasta and water into the colander as soon as the pasta is done.

13

Homemade Pasta

Preparation Time: 1¼ hours

INGREDIENTS

2 CUPS ALL-PURPOSE FLOUR
1/2 TEASPOON SALT
2 BEATEN EGGS
1/3 CUP WATER
1 TEASPOON OLIVE OIL *OR* COOKING OIL
1/3 CUP ALL-PURPOSE FLOUR

*T*his simple dough can be used for every recipe in this book that calls for fresh pasta. Although quick to prepare, to save more time you can make the dough ahead and freeze (see the tip box on page 9 for freezing and thawing directions). To substitute fresh pasta in a recipe that specifies dried, use 8 ounces fresh for every 4 ounces of dried pasta.

■ In a large mixing bowl stir together the 2 cups flour and the salt. Make a well in the center of the mixture.

■ In a small mixing bowl stir together the eggs, water, and olive oil or cooking oil. Add to the flour mixture and mix well.

■ Sprinkle kneading surface with the ⅓ cup flour. (Spinach, whole-wheat, and tomato variations may not require the addition of any or all of this flour.) Turn dough out onto floured surface. Knead till dough is smooth and elastic (8 to 10 minutes total). Cover and let rest for 10 minutes.

■ Divide dough into fourths. On a lightly floured surface, roll each fourth into a 12-inch square about ¹⁄₁₆ inch thick. Let stand about 20 minutes, or till slightly dry. Or, if using a pasta machine, pass each fourth of dough through machine, according to manufacturer's directions, till ¹⁄₁₆ inch thick. Shape or stuff as desired, or as directed in recipe.

■ To dry ribbons, hang pasta from a pasta-drying rack or clothes hanger, or toss with flour, shape into loose bundles, and place on a floured baking sheet. Let dry overnight or till completely dry. Place in an airtight container and refrigerate up to 3 days. Or, dry the pasta at least 1 hour. Seal it in a freezer bag or container. Freeze for up to 8 months.

Makes 4 portions pasta (1 pound total)

■ **For Herb Pasta,** prepare pasta as directed, *except* add 1 teaspoon *dried basil, marjoram, or sage,* crushed, to flour mixture.

■ **For Spinach Pasta,** prepare pasta as directed, *except* decrease the water to 3 tablespoons and add ⅓ cup very finely chopped cooked *spinach,* well drained, to the egg mixture.

■ **For Whole-Wheat Pasta,** prepare pasta as directed, *except* substitute *whole-wheat flour* for the all-purpose flour.

■ **For Tomato Pasta,** prepare pasta as directed, *except* substitute *tomato paste* for the water.

Per portion plain pasta: 292 calories, 10 g protein, 51 g carbohydrate, 4 g total fat (1 g saturated), 107 mg cholesterol, 300 mg sodium, 102 mg potassium

14

Basic Sauces

Steps for Preparing Sauce Ingredients

BASIC TOOLS FOR PREPARING SAUCE INGREDIENTS

Use knives and kitchen scissors to peel, slice, or chop vegetables and snip leafy herbs. Specialty tools include a press
for mincing garlic and a grater with fine holes for Parmesan.
A colander, bowl, and measuring cup hold ingredients.

COLANDER

CUTTING BOARD, PARMESAN
GRATER, AND GARLIC PRESS

SMALL BOWL

MEASURING
CUP

SCISSORS

CHEF'S KNIFE

SMALL, SHARP KNIFE

16

Favorite sauces for pasta range from the simplicity of
garlic-infused olive oil or melted butter — for which
no recipe is even needed — to herbal pestos and rich, complex concoctions of cream, cheese, and eggs. Tomatoes
and pasta are a classic pairing with endless uses. In this
chapter, you'll find a selection of basic sauces that can
be served over your favorite hot cooked pasta or used as
directed in other recipes in this book.

As with all dishes, a pasta sauce is only as good as
what you put into it. For red sauces, fully ripened fresh
plum tomatoes are best. They are meaty and juicy, not
watery, and cook down into a thicker mixture. If they
aren't available, canned plum tomatoes (sometimes
labeled "Italian-style tomatoes") are preferable to fresh
ones that are unripe or flavorless. Fresh herbs, whether
basil, parsley, or oregano, should look lively, not wilted,
while dried herbs should be less than 6 months old and
have a characteristic aroma. Finally, there is no compari-
son between Parmesan, or other hard cheese, hand-grated
from a fresh wedge and packaged grated cheese. Resist the
temptation to use pre-grated cheeses and you'll find your
sauces taste better than ever.

in the boiling
water, the
tomato skin
will split at
the X and peel
away easily

STEP 1 PEELING TOMATOES

Cut an X in the blossom end of the tomato with the point
of a knife, then plunge the tomato into boiling water for
20 to 30 seconds to loosen the skin. Transfer to a colander to drain. When cool enough to handle, peel off the
skin by pulling it away with a small, sharp knife.

stubborn seeds can also be coaxed out with a knife or your finger

STEP 2 SEEDING TOMATOES

Cut the peeled tomato in half crosswise with a sharp knife. Hold the cut half upside down over the sink and squeeze gently to force out most of the seeds.

if the recipe calls for drained tomatoes, pour into a sieve, then cut up

STEP 3 CUTTING UP CANNED TOMATOES

Insert a pair of sharp kitchen scissors with long blades into the can of whole tomatoes (no need to drain off the juice). Open and close the blades to cut the tomatoes into small pieces. Or, pour tomatoes into a bowl and then cut up.

to grate a large amount of Parmesan cheese, drop chunks into a running food processor fitted with a metal blade

STEP 4 GRATING FRESH PARMESAN

Rub a chunk of fresh Parmesan cheese across the holes of a hand grater. If you grate fresh cheese often, you may want to purchase a hand-turned crank-style grater that you can bring to the table.

17

you can also chop delicate herbs with a knife, but snipping is gentler and there is less chance of mashing the leaves

STEP 5 SNIPPING FRESH HERBS

Strip the leaves of fresh herbs from their stems. Discard the stems and place the leaves in a measuring cup or bowl. Snip into small pieces with kitchen scissors.

you can also mince garlic with a knife

STEP 6 MINCING GARLIC

Remove a clove of garlic from the head. Peel away the papery skin unless your garlic press will mince cloves with the skin intact. Squeeze the arms of the press together to force the garlic through the holes into a bowl.

grip the onion half with your fingers to keep it steady

STEP 7 CHOPPING ONIONS

Halve the onion lengthwise. Place one half, cut-side down, on a work surface. With a sharp knife, make a series of horizontal cuts almost to the root end and parallel to the work surface. Then make a series of evenly spaced vertical cuts from the top of the onion to the work surface. Finally, slice across the onion to create pieces.

Classic Tomato Sauce

Preparation Time: 40 minutes
Cooking Time: 25 minutes

INGREDIENTS

4	POUNDS RIPE PLUM TOMATOES *OR* THREE 14-1/2-OUNCE CANS WHOLE ITALIAN-STYLE TOMATOES
2	TABLESPOONS OLIVE OIL *OR* COOKING OIL
2	CLOVES GARLIC, MINCED
1/2	TEASPOON SALT
1/2	TEASPOON SUGAR
1/4	TEASPOON PEPPER
1/3	CUP SNIPPED FRESH BASIL, OREGANO, *OR* PARSLEY

*I*f you like your tomato sauce chunky, skip the blending or processing step and serve it hot from the pan. If you like, add meatballs to the sauce (see recipe, page 46).

■ Peel, seed, and finely chop the fresh plum tomatoes, if using. In a large saucepan or Dutch oven, heat olive oil or cooking oil over medium heat. Add fresh or undrained canned tomatoes, garlic, salt (omit if using canned tomatoes), sugar, and pepper. Bring to boiling; reduce heat. Simmer, uncovered, for about 20 minutes, or to desired consistency. Place about half of the sauce in a food processor bowl or blender container; process or blend till smooth. Return blended tomato mixture to saucepan. Stir in basil, oregano, or parsley. Cook for 5 minutes more.

Makes about 4 cups

Per cup: 160 calories, 4 g protein, 22 g carbohydrate, 8 g total fat (1 g saturated), 0 mg cholesterol, 308 mg sodium, 1,030 mg potassium

18

STEPS FOR MAKING TOMATO SAUCE

STEP 1 SIMMERING SAUCE

To achieve the desired consistency, bring the sauce ingredients to a boil, then reduce the heat and simmer uncovered, stirring now and then. This allows the excess liquid to evaporate and the flavors to become concentrated. When the tomatoes are broken down and the sauce is no longer runny, the sauce is done.

STEP 2 BLENDING SAUCE

Purée about half of the sauce in a blender or food processor. Return to the saucepan; add snipped herbs (fresh herbs are added at the last minute to preserve their fresh flavor). Cook 5 minutes more.

All pasta cooks should have a basic tomato sauce in their repertoire and a supply ready-made in the freezer to use at a moment's notice.

The ancient city of Bologna, Italy, gave its name to a flavorful meat sauce that makes a hearty meal when combined with any pasta shape. Italians also call the sauce *ragù*.

Bolognese Sauce

Preparation Time: 30 minutes
Cooking Time: 38 to 40 minutes

INGREDIENTS

2	POUNDS RIPE PLUM TOMATOES OR TWO 14-1/2-OUNCE CANS WHOLE ITALIAN-STYLE TOMATOES, DRAINED
12	OUNCES LEAN GROUND BEEF
1	CUP FINELY CHOPPED ONION
1/2	CUP FINELY CHOPPED CARROT
1/2	CUP FINELY CHOPPED CELERY
2	SLICES BACON, FINELY CHOPPED
1/2	CUP DRY RED WINE
3/4	CUP WHIPPING CREAM
1/2	TEASPOON SALT
1/4	TEASPOON PEPPER
1/8	TEASPOON GROUND NUTMEG

*E*xperiment with substituting Italian sausage, turkey sausage, or smoked sausage for the ground beef, or use a combination of veal and pork which is the mark of a traditional Bolognese sauce.

■ Peel and seed fresh plum tomatoes, if using. In a food processor bowl or blender container process or blend fresh or canned tomatoes till smooth; set aside.

■ In a large skillet cook ground beef, onion, carrot, celery, and bacon for 5 minutes, or till meat is brown and vegetables are tender, stirring to break the meat into tiny pieces. Drain off fat. Add the wine. Bring to boiling; reduce heat. Simmer, uncovered, for 3 to 5 minutes, or till nearly all of the liquid has evaporated, stirring occasionally.

■ Stir in tomatoes. Cover and simmer for 30 minutes, or to desired consistency, stirring occasionally. Stir in whipping cream, salt (omit if using canned tomatoes), pepper, and nutmeg. Heat through.

Makes 4 cups

Per cup: 436 calories, 21 g protein, 22 g carbohydrate, 29 g total fat (15 g saturated), 117 mg cholesterol, 428 mg sodium, 1,069 mg potassium

21

STEPS FOR MAKING BOLOGNESE SAUCE

STEP 1 GRATING NUTMEG
Rub a whole nutmeg across the grating holes of a nutmeg grater. Work over a piece of waxed paper or a bowl to collect the grated spice. Packaged ground nutmeg is an acceptable substitute for fresh, but it won't be as aromatic or flavorful.

STEP 2 BROWNING MEAT
Cook the meat until it is brown and the vegetables are tender, stirring with a wooden spoon to break the ground meat into little pieces.

STEP 3 ADDING CREAM
Cream is added last to thicken and enrich the sauce. Pour it in while stirring to keep the cream from boiling over. Stir to blend thoroughly and cook a few minutes more to heat through.

Pesto

Preparation Time: 15 minutes

INGREDIENTS

1-1/2	CUPS FIRMLY PACKED FRESH BASIL LEAVES
1/4	CUP GRATED PARMESAN CHEESE
1/4	CUP GRATED ROMANO CHEESE
1/4	CUP PINE NUTS *OR* SLIVERED ALMONDS
1	LARGE CLOVE GARLIC, SLICED
1/8	TEASPOON SALT
1/4	CUP OLIVE OIL *OR* COOKING OIL

A little pesto has a lot of flavor, so for a simple side dish, plan on using about ¼ cup of pesto tossed with 4 ounces dried or 8 ounces fresh pasta, cooked and drained.

■ In a food processor bowl or blender container combine basil, Parmesan cheese, Romano cheese, pine nuts or almonds, garlic, and salt. Pour in olive oil or cooking oil. Cover and process or blend with several on/off turns till a purée forms, stopping the machine several times and cleaning the sides with a rubber spatula. Store any remaining pesto in ¼-cup portions, wrapped and frozen for up to 1 year or refrigerated for up to 2 days. Before using, bring to room temperature.

Makes ¾ cup

Per tablespoon: 98 calories, 3 g protein, 1 g carbohydrate, 8 g total fat (2 g saturated), 4 mg cholesterol, 89 mg sodium, 74 mg potassium

STEPS FOR MAKING PESTO

STEP 1 **ADDING INGREDIENTS**
Pour oil over the other pesto ingredients. The work bowl of the food processor should be fitted with the metal blade.

STEP 2 **FINISHING SAUCE**
Process with a few on/off pulses until a purée forms. Scrape down the sides of the work bowl a few times between pulses to blend.

STEP 3 **STORING SAUCE**
Spoon ¼-cup portions into small freezer or refrigerator containers. Before securing the lid, cover the pesto surface with plastic wrap to prevent browning. The sauce will keep, frozen, for up to 1 year.

Smooth, fragrant pesto coats strands
of pasta with the incomparable flavor
of fresh-picked basil.

Marinara Sauce

Preparation Time: 20 minutes
Cooking Time: 20 to 25 minutes

INGREDIENTS

8	OUNCES FRESH MUSHROOMS, THINLY SLICED (3 CUPS)
1/2	CUP CHOPPED ONION
2	CLOVES GARLIC, MINCED
1	TABLESPOON OLIVE OIL *OR* COOKING OIL
2	CUPS SHREDDED ZUCCHINI
1	15-OUNCE CAN TOMATO SAUCE WITH TOMATO BITS
1/2	CUP DRY RED WINE
1	TABLESPOON SNIPPED FRESH SAGE
1/4	TEASPOON SALT
1/4	TEASPOON PEPPER

24

This sauce is chunkier and more complex than a simple tomato sauce. Red wine adds body, and sliced mushrooms and shredded zucchini give the sauce texture and depth of flavor.

*T*his *traditional Italian sauce is never made with meat. Spoon it over hot cooked pasta and sprinkle with a little feta cheese or Parmesan cheese for a scrumptious vegetarian dish.*

■ In a large skillet cook mushrooms, onion, and garlic in hot olive oil or cooking oil for 5 minutes, stirring constantly. Add zucchini and cook for 5 minutes, or till vegetables are tender but not brown. Add tomato sauce, wine, sage, salt, and pepper. Bring to boiling; reduce heat. Simmer, uncovered, for 10 to 15 minutes, or to desired consistency, stirring frequently. *Makes 4 cups*

Per cup: 115 calories, 3 g protein, 15 g carbohydrate, 4 g total fat (1 g saturated), 0 mg cholesterol, 798 mg sodium, 785 mg potassium

Hearty Sausage & Tomato Sauce

*A*djust the level of heat to your liking by selecting either sweet or hot Italian sausage. Besides serving this sauce over pasta, you could also use it as a base for a hot and spicy chili.

■ Peel, seed, and chop the fresh plum tomatoes, if using.

■ In a large saucepan cook the Italian sausage, onion, green pepper, and garlic for 5 minutes, or till sausage is brown. Drain off fat. Carefully stir in the fresh or undrained canned tomatoes, tomato paste, salt, oregano, basil, pepper, and red pepper. Bring to boiling; reduce heat. Cover and simmer for 30 minutes. Then uncover and simmer for 10 to 15 minutes more, or to desired consistency, stirring occasionally.

Makes 4 cups

Per cup: 313 calories, 17 g protein, 25 g carbohydrate, 17 g total fat (6 g saturated), 49 mg cholesterol, 898 mg sodium, 1,274 mg potassium

INGREDIENTS

2	POUNDS RIPE PLUM TOMATOES OR TWO 14-1/2-OUNCE CANS WHOLE ITALIAN-STYLE TOMATOES, CUT UP
12	OUNCES BULK ITALIAN SAUSAGE
1/2	CUP CHOPPED ONION
1/4	CUP FINELY CHOPPED GREEN SWEET PEPPER
2	CLOVES GARLIC, MINCED
1	6-OUNCE CAN TOMATO PASTE
1/2	TEASPOON SALT
1/2	TEASPOON DRIED OREGANO, CRUSHED
1/2	TEASPOON DRIED BASIL, CRUSHED
1/4	TEASPOON PEPPER
1/4	TEASPOON GROUND RED PEPPER

Preparation Time: 30 minutes
Cooking Time: 45 to 50 minutes

Pair this robust meat sauce with an equally substantial pasta such as penne.

Creamy Parmesan Sauce

Preparation Time: 50 minutes
Cooking Time: 2 to 10 minutes

INGREDIENTS

1/3	CUP HALF-AND-HALF *OR* WHIPPING CREAM
2	TABLESPOONS MARGARINE *OR* BUTTER
4	OUNCES DRIED *OR* 8 OUNCES FRESH TOMATO, HERB, *OR* PLAIN FETTUCCINE
1/3	CUP GRATED PARMESAN CHEESE
1/4	TEASPOON SALT
1	SMALL CLOVE GARLIC, MINCED
1	TABLESPOON SNIPPED FRESH BASIL *OR* SNIPPED FRESH PARSLEY (OPTIONAL)
	COARSELY GROUND BLACK PEPPER (OPTIONAL)

*C*ombine this rich cheese sauce with pasta ribbons and you have the classic pasta dish, *fettuccine Alfredo. As the sauce is poured over the cooked pasta, the heat cooks the sauce, causing the cream to thicken slightly and the cheese to melt.*

■ Allow half-and-half or whipping cream and margarine or butter to come to room temperature (about 40 minutes).

■ In a large saucepan or pasta pot bring 3 quarts water to boiling. Add pasta. Reduce heat slightly. Boil, uncovered, for 8 to 10 minutes for dried pasta or 1½ to 2 minutes for fresh pasta, or till al dente, stirring occasionally. (Or, cook according to package directions.) Immediately drain.

■ Return pasta to the warm pan. Add Parmesan cheese, half-and-half or whipping cream, margarine or butter, salt, and garlic. Toss gently till pasta is well coated. Transfer to a warm serving dish. If desired, sprinkle with basil or parsley and pepper. Serve immediately.

Makes 4 side-dish or 2 main-dish servings

Per serving: 282 calories, 10 g protein, 35 g carbohydrate, 11 g total fat (4 g saturated), 13 mg cholesterol, 363 mg sodium, 78 mg potassium

26

Fresh tomato pasta provides a subtle contrast to this rich and creamy cheese sauce. Serve alongside a favorite chop and fresh vegetable.

Ribbon Pasta

Steps for Cutting Ribbon Pasta

BASIC TOOLS FOR MAKING RIBBON PASTA

Cut sheets of fresh pasta into ribbons with a small, sharp knife or with a pasta machine. To dry, drape the noodles over the rods of a pasta drying rack or arrange them in a shallow baking pan.

PASTA DRYING RACK

CUTTING BOARD AND SHALLOW BAKING PAN

28

PASTA MACHINE

SMALL, SHARP KNIFE

AMONG THE MOST VERSATILE of all pastas are the silken, flat ribbons cut from fresh dough. Called by a variety of names, depending on the width of the noodle, all ribbon pastas are superb with creamy sauces, pesto, and tomato-based sauces.

Homemade pasta ribbons with straight edges can be cut with a sharp knife or with the roller blades of a pasta machine (only a commercial machine will produce ribbons with ruffled edges). The cutting blades of a hand-cranked pasta machine are preset to two prescribed sizes: $1/4$ inch wide for fettuccine or $1/16$ inch wide for fine noodles — a similar size to spaghetti. When you cut the dough with a knife, the strips can be the traditional widths or any that appeal to you, including wide lasagne (see page 76).

After you have made the dough and rolled it out (see pages 9 and 11), it must rest on a towel, uncovered, for about 20 minutes to allow the surface to dry slightly. This step keeps the pasta from sticking when it is rolled and sliced with a knife or when it is fed through the machine. If the sheets are very long, cut them into a manageable length.

The steps opposite show how to create ribbons by cutting a sheet of rolled dough with a knife or with a hand-cranked pasta machine. After you have cut the ribbons by either method, the pasta can dry for up to 1 hour before it is cooked. You can drape it over the dowels of a special wooden pasta rack, or wrap it into little nests and place in a lightly floured shallow baking pan. If the pasta will not be used immediately, let it dry completely, preferably overnight. Once dried, place it in an airtight container and store in the refrigerator for up to 3 days. To freeze for up to 8 months, let the ribbons dry for 1 hour, then seal in a freezer bag or container.

Homemade pasta that has been fully dried can be used interchangeably with packaged dried pasta in the recipes in this book. If cooking homemade ribbons right away, follow the directions given for *fresh* pasta.

rolling the dough into a tube makes it easier to slice into uniform ribbons

STEP 1   ROLLING UP DOUGH

After the surface of the thin dough sheet has dried slightly, roll up the sheet loosely like a jelly roll. Don't squeeze the roll or the dough might stick together.

if your knife is dull it will compress the roll rather than slice it cleanly

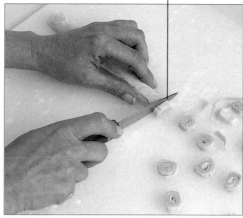

STEP 2   CUTTING DOUGH

Be sure your knife is very sharp. Slice the rolled dough into ¼-inch-wide strips for fettuccine, ⅛-inch-wide strips for linguine, or any width desired. For lasagne, cut the dough into 2½-inch-wide strips.

turn the handle clockwise only or the sheets won't pass through the blades

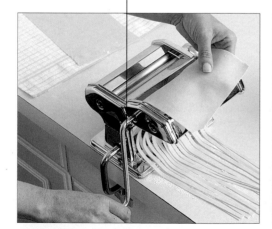

STEP 3   MACHINE-CUTTING FETTUCCINE

Secure the cutting attachment to the machine. If necessary, cut the rolled pasta sheet in half to match the width of the machine. Feed the pasta sheet through the ¼-inch-wide cutters.

to make ribbons of the same length, be sure the sheet is fed through evenly

STEP 4   MACHINE-CUTTING FINE STRANDS

To make narrower strands, simply feed the rolled pasta sheet through the fine cutters, rather than the wider fettuccine blades. The fine strands will be more delicate than fettuccine, so handle them carefully. Use as you would spaghetti.

TIP BOX

DRYING PASTA

STEP 1   RACK DRYING

Loosely gather the ribbons and hang them on the dowels of a pasta-drying rack. A pound of ribbons should fit on most standard racks.

separate the strands so they won't stick together

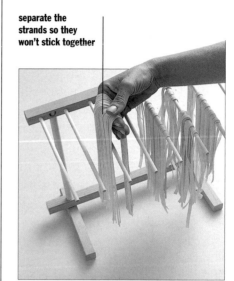

29

STEP 2   DRYING ON A BAKING SHEET

Toss the pasta ribbons in flour and loosely shape into bundles. Arrange in a flour-dusted baking pan to dry.

use a metal baking sheet or jelly-roll pan

Dried Pasta Ribbons and Strands

I N THE COMPLICATED HIERARCHY of Italian ribbon-pasta nomenclature, almost infinitesimal differences in width result in a different pasta. Names can also differ from one part of Italy to the other (for example, ¼-inch-wide ribbons are called fettuccine in most regions, except in parts of the north where they are called tagliatelle), or from manufacturer to manufacturer. If a recipe calls for a particular ribbon and you can't find it in the store, be assured that you will come across another that is very similar to the one you need and that will work just as well. The best dried pasta is made from semolina flour or durum flour, both ground from hard durum wheat. Unlike fresh ribbon pasta, dried ribbon pasta may take the form of long, narrow rods (spaghetti and vermicelli), twisted strands (fusilli), or ruffled ribbons (mafalde).

Ribbon pastas also appear throughout Asia. While dried Italian pasta is made with flour, water, and sometimes egg, Asian noodles use wheat, buckwheat, and rice flours, or vegetable starches made from beans or potatoes. Some incorporate egg, while others don't. Packaged Asian pastas are available at Asian markets and some supermarkets.

you may want to reserve some sauce to pass at the table

STEP 1 TOSSING PASTA

Use a large bowl to allow plenty of room for tossing. Warm the bowl first to keep the pasta hot. Add about half of the sauce; toss to coat the strands, then add the remaining sauce and toss again.

Here's a look at some of the most widely available dried pasta ribbons and strands. Although similar, each is different enough to add its own unique character to a dish. Buckwheat noodles (soba) and pancit canton noodles are used in Asian dishes.

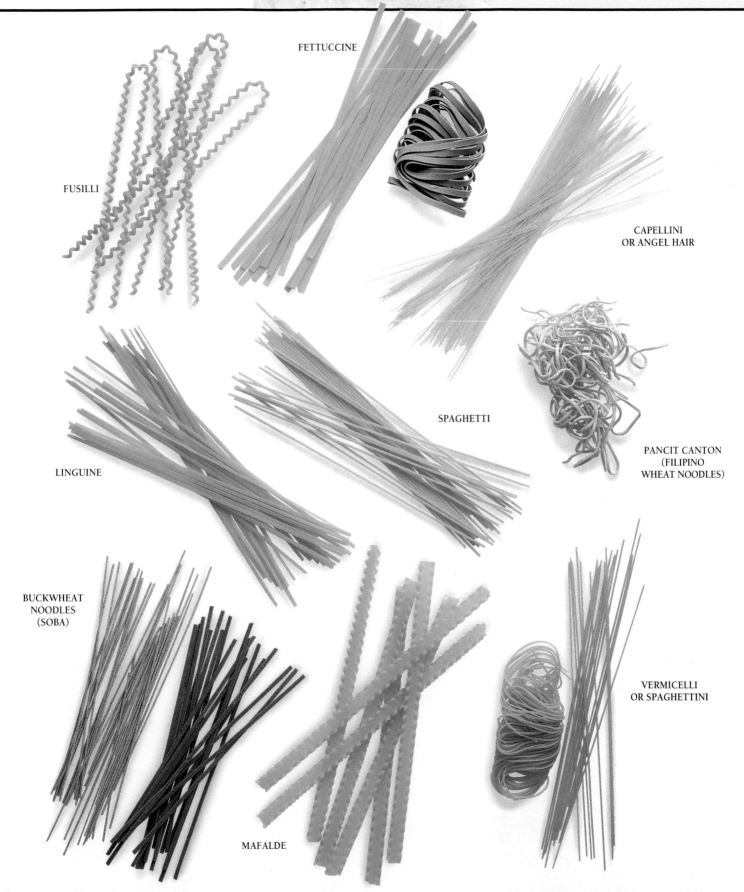

FETTUCCINE

FUSILLI

CAPELLINI
OR ANGEL HAIR

SPAGHETTI

PANCIT CANTON
(FILIPINO
WHEAT NOODLES)

LINGUINE

BUCKWHEAT
NOODLES
(SOBA)

VERMICELLI
OR SPAGHETTINI

MAFALDE

Fettuccine with Sweet & Sour Vegetables

Preparation Time: 20 minutes
Cooking Time: 28 to 30 minutes

INGREDIENTS

3	CUPS KALE, COLLARD GREENS, OR SPINACH
6	OUNCES YELLOW SUMMER SQUASH, CUT INTO 1/4-INCH-THICK SLICES (1-1/2 CUPS)
4	OUNCES DRIED FETTUCCINE OR LINGUINE, OR 8 OUNCES FRESH FETTUCCINE OR LINGUINE
1	OUNCE PANCETTA OR THICK-SLICED BACON, FINELY CHOPPED
2	TABLESPOONS OLIVE OIL OR COOKING OIL
1/2	CUP CHOPPED ONION
1	TABLESPOON ALL-PURPOSE FLOUR
1	TABLESPOON SUGAR
1/2	TEASPOON SALT
1/8	TEASPOON PEPPER
3/4	CUP CHICKEN BROTH
1/4	CUP RED WINE VINEGAR

*I*f you decide to use spinach instead of kale or collard greens, take note that it cooks in much less time. Start by cooking the pasta, then cook the vegetables and sauce.

■ Wash the greens. Remove center ribs, if necessary, and tear each leaf into bite-size pieces. In a large saucepan bring 1 cup water to boiling. Add the kale or collard greens (if using) and simmer, covered, for 25 minutes. Add summer squash and spinach (if using) and cook for 3 to 5 minutes more, or till vegetables are tender. Drain and keep warm.

■ Meanwhile, in a large saucepan or pasta pot bring 3 quarts water to boiling. Add pasta. Reduce heat slightly. Boil, uncovered, for 8 to 10 minutes for dried pasta or 1½ to 2 minutes for fresh pasta, or till al dente, stirring occasionally. (Or, cook according to package directions.) Immediately drain.

■ Meanwhile, in a large skillet cook the pancetta in hot oil. (If using bacon, cook it without the oil.) Add onion to cooked pancetta or bacon and cook till tender. Stir in flour, sugar, salt, and pepper. Stir in chicken broth and vinegar all at once. Cook and stir till thickened and bubbly. Cook and stir for 2 minutes more. Stir in cooked greens and squash; mix well. Serve greens mixture over hot cooked pasta. Serve immediately.

Makes 4 side-dish servings

Per serving: 255 calories, 8 g protein, 31 g carbohydrate, 11 g total fat (4 g saturated), 12 mg cholesterol, 535 mg sodium, 249 mg potassium

STEPS AT A GLANCE	Page
MAKING PASTA	8–14
CUTTING RIBBON PASTA	28
PREPARING MEAT & VEGETABLES	32

32

STEPS FOR PREPARING MEAT AND VEGETABLES

STEP 1 PREPARING GREENS
Cut along either side of the center rib of kale or collard greens from top to bottom; discard the ribs.

STEP 2 DICING PANCETTA
Make parallel cuts in one flat slice of pancetta. Turn the knife and slice across the cuts to form diced pieces.

STEP 3 COOKING PANCETTA
Heat the oil, then add the diced pancetta. Cook until browned and crisp on the edges, tossing to keep the pieces from sticking.

Pancetta, a spiced, unsmoked Italian bacon, seasons this tangy sweet-and-sour sauce brightened with kale and summer squash.

Strands of pasta twine around a
colorful mixture of vegetables, all
coated with a creamy sauce.

34

Springtime Carbonara

Preparation Time: 20 minutes
Cooking Time: 18 to 19 minutes

INGREDIENTS

1	CUP BABY CARROTS (4 OUNCES)
1	CUP LOOSE-PACK FROZEN PEAS OR SHELLED FRESH PEAS
4	OUNCES FRESH ASPARAGUS, TRIMMED AND CUT INTO 2-INCH PIECES (3/4 CUP)
6	OUNCES DRIED SPAGHETTI OR FETTUCCINE OR 12 OUNCES FRESH FETTUCCINE OR OTHER RIBBON PASTA
1	BEATEN EGG
1	CUP HALF-AND-HALF OR LIGHT CREAM
2	TABLESPOONS MARGARINE OR BUTTER
1/2	CUP GRATED PARMESAN CHEESE
2	TABLESPOONS SNIPPED FRESH CHIVES OR GREEN ONIONS
	PEPPER

We call this "springtime" because vegetables replace the bacon used in traditional carbonara. However, with fresh vegetables available year-round, you can enjoy this delicious carbonara during the winter, too.

■ In a medium saucepan cook carrots in a small amount of boiling water for 10 minutes. Add peas and asparagus. Cook for 5 minutes more, or till vegetables are crisp-tender. Drain.

■ Meanwhile, in a large saucepan or pasta pot bring 3 quarts water to boiling. Add pasta. Reduce heat slightly. Boil, uncovered, 8 to 12 minutes for dried pasta or 1½ to 2 minutes for fresh, or till al dente, stirring occasionally. (Or, cook according to package directions.) Return pasta to warm pan; add cooked vegetables.

■ In a medium saucepan combine the egg, half-and-half or light cream, and margarine or butter. Cook and stir over medium heat till mixture just coats a metal spoon (about 3 to 4 minutes). Remove from heat. Immediately stir in the Parmesan cheese and chives or green onions. Pour egg mixture over hot pasta and vegetables and toss to coat pasta. Transfer to a warm serving dish. Sprinkle with pepper. Serve immediately.

Makes 6 side-dish servings

Per serving: 276 calories, 11 g protein, 31 g carbohydrate, 12 g total fat (7 g saturated), 65 mg cholesterol, 229 mg sodium, 257 mg potassium

STEPS FOR MAKING CARBONARA SAUCE

STEP 1 TESTING EGG MIXTURE

Dip a spoon into the cooked egg mixture. The excess should drip off, leaving a creamy coating slightly thicker than milk. The coating should hold its shape when you wipe a finger across the back of the spoon.

STEP 2 SNIPPING CHIVES

Hold a bunch of chives with one hand (remove any damaged pieces). With kitchen scissors, snip off little tubes (about ¼ inch long) into a small bowl.

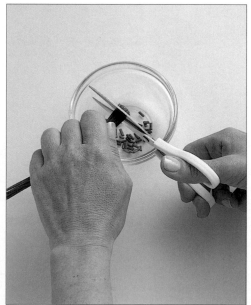

Pasta & Shrimp Diavolo

Preparation Time: 25 minutes
Cooking Time: 8 to 12 minutes

INGREDIENTS

8	OUNCES DRIED SPAGHETTI, LINGUINE, *OR* FETTUCCINE *OR* 1 POUND FRESH FETTUCCINE *OR* LINGUINE
2	CUPS BROCCOLI FLOWERETS
1	CUP CHICKEN BROTH
2	TABLESPOONS CORNSTARCH
2	TABLESPOONS DIJON-STYLE MUSTARD
2	TABLESPOONS LEMON JUICE
1	TABLESPOON DRAINED CAPERS
1	POUND FRESH SHRIMP, PEELED AND DEVEINED, *OR* 12 OUNCES FROZEN PEELED AND DEVEINED SHRIMP, THAWED
2	TABLESPOONS OLIVE OIL *OR* COOKING OIL
1/2	TEASPOON HOT CHILI OIL
	LEMON WEDGES (OPTIONAL)

*Y*ou can easily adjust the spiciness of this dish by increasing or decreasing the amount of hot chili oil you use, or by adding crushed red pepper for a real kick.

■ In a large saucepan or pasta pot bring 3 quarts water to boiling. Add pasta. Reduce heat slightly. Boil, uncovered, 8 to 12 minutes for dried pasta or 1½ to 2 minutes for fresh, or till al dente, stirring occasionally. (Or, cook according to package directions.) Add the broccoli to the boiling dried pasta during the last 5 minutes of cooking time. Immediately drain. (If using fresh pasta, cook the broccoli separately in a small amount of boiling water for about 5 minutes, or until crisp-tender. Drain and add to cooked pasta.)

■ Meanwhile, in a small mixing bowl stir together chicken broth, cornstarch, mustard, lemon juice, and capers; set aside. In a large skillet cook and stir shrimp in hot olive oil or cooking oil and chili oil over medium-high heat for 1 minute. Stir broth mixture; carefully add to skillet. Cook and stir till thickened and bubbly. Cook and stir for 2 minutes more, or till shrimp turn pink. Toss with pasta-broccoli mixture. If desired, garnish with lemon wedges. Serve immediately.

Makes 4 main-dish servings

Per serving: 407 calories, 25 g protein, 51 g carbohydrate, 11 g total fat (2 g saturated), 131 mg cholesterol, 588 mg sodium, 408 mg potassium

36

STEPS FOR MAKING SHRIMP DIAVOLO

STEP 1 CUTTING FLOWERETS
Flowerets are the tightly closed heads that top each thick stalk of broccoli. Trim off the stalks and use them in another recipe. Halve or quarter the flowerets if large.

STEP 2 PEELING SHRIMP
With kitchen scissors or a paring knife, cut the shell along the curve of the back from head to tail end. The shell and legs should peel off in one piece. To devein, pull out and discard the dark vein that runs along the back.

STEP 3 COOKING SHRIMP
Add the broth mixture to the partially cooked shrimp in the skillet. Cook and stir an additional 2 minutes, or until the shrimp turn pink and opaque.

Diavolo is synonymous with "spicy." In this quick-to-assemble seafood dish, mustard and chili oil provide the heat.

Tarragon and pungent blue-veined
Gorgonzola add punch to this creamy
sauce. A garnish of chopped toasted
pecans provides a crunchy counterpoint.

Fettuccine with Gorgonzola-Tarragon Sauce

This pasta dish is rich with cream and the intense flavor of Gorgonzola. Pass some extra crumbled Gorgonzola with the pasta for the cheese-lovers at the table.

■ In a large saucepan or pasta pot bring 3 quarts water to boiling. Add pasta. Reduce heat slightly. Boil, uncovered, 8 to 10 minutes for dried pasta or 1½ to 2 minutes for fresh, or till al dente, stirring occasionally. (Or, cook according to package directions.) Immediately drain. Return pasta to warm pan.

■ Meanwhile, in a small saucepan melt margarine or butter. Add the Gorgonzola cheese, half-and-half or light cream, tarragon, and pepper. Cook and stir over medium heat till cheese is melted and mixture is smooth and heated through. Stir in Parmesan cheese. Pour sauce over pasta. Gently toss till pasta is coated. Transfer to a warm serving dish. Sprinkle with nuts. Serve immediately.

Makes 4 side-dish servings

Per serving: 253 calories, 10 g protein, 23 g carbohydrate, 13 g total fat (7 g saturated), 29 mg cholesterol, 377 mg sodium, 130 mg potassium

Preparation Time: 15 minutes
Cooking Time: 8 to 10 minutes

INGREDIENTS

4	OUNCES DRIED *OR* 8 OUNCES FRESH SPINACH FETTUCCINE *OR* LINGUINE
1	TABLESPOON MARGARINE *OR* BUTTER
1/2	CUP CRUMBLED GORGONZOLA CHEESE (2 OUNCES)
1/4	CUP HALF-AND-HALF *OR* LIGHT CREAM
2	TABLESPOONS SNIPPED FRESH TARRAGON *OR* 1-1/2 TEASPOONS DRIED TARRAGON, CRUSHED
	DASH GROUND WHITE PEPPER *OR* BLACK PEPPER
1/4	CUP GRATED PARMESAN CHEESE
2	TABLESPOONS CHOPPED TOASTED PECANS *OR* WALNUTS

39

STEPS FOR CRUMBLING CHEESE AND TOASTING NUTS

STEP 1 CRUMBLING GORGONZOLA
In order for the cheese to melt quickly and smoothly, it should be crumbled first. Put a chunk of cheese in a pie plate or on a dish. Crumble by breaking it up with a fork.

STEP 2 TOASTING NUTS
Spread the nuts in a metal pie pan. Bake in a preheated 350° oven for 5 to 10 minutes, or until lightly browned. Stir once or twice so the nuts brown evenly.

Aglio e Olio with Fresh Sage

STEPS AT A GLANCE	Page
MAKING PASTA	8–14
CUTTING RIBBON PASTA	28

Preparation Time: 10 minutes
Cooking Time: 10 to 12 minutes

INGREDIENTS

4	OUNCES MAFALDE, SPAGHETTI, *OR* OTHER DRIED RIBBON PASTA *OR* 8 OUNCES FRESH FETTUCCINE
2	TABLESPOONS OLIVE OIL *OR* COOKING OIL
2	CLOVES GARLIC, MINCED
1	TABLESPOON SNIPPED FRESH SAGE *OR* 1/2 TEASPOON DRIED SAGE, CRUSHED
	SALT AND PEPPER
	GRATED PARMESAN CHEESE (OPTIONAL)

40

Accompany roasted or grilled chicken with ruffled ribbon pasta in a garlicky sauce flecked with bits of sage.

*G*arlic (aglio) and oil (olio) are a classic Italian combination. When sage is added, you have a light and delicious pasta sauce that can be made in a snap.

■ In a large saucepan or pasta pot bring 3 quarts water to boiling. Add pasta. Reduce heat slightly. Boil, uncovered, for 10 to 12 minutes for dried pasta or 1½ to 2 minutes for fresh, or till al dente, stirring occasionally. (Or, cook according to package directions.) Immediately drain. Return pasta to warm pan.

■ Meanwhile, in a small saucepan heat oil over medium heat. Add garlic and sage and cook and stir for 1 minute.

■ Toss sage mixture with hot pasta. Season to taste with salt and pepper. If desired, sprinkle with Parmesan cheese. Serve immediately.

Makes 4 side-dish servings

Per serving: 175 calories, 4 g protein, 23 g carbohydrate, 7 g total fat (1 g saturated), 0 mg cholesterol, 35 mg sodium, 32 mg potassium

Straw & Hay with Wild Mushrooms in Cream

*P*our *a little of the boiling water from the pasta pot into your serving bowl to heat it up quickly. Empty the water just before you are ready to fill the bowl with pasta.*

■ In a large saucepan or pasta pot bring 3 quarts water to boiling. Add pasta. Reduce heat slightly. Boil, uncovered, for 8 to 10 minutes for dried pasta or 1½ to 2 minutes for fresh, or till al dente, stirring occasionally. (Or, cook according to package directions.) Immediately drain. Return pasta to warm pan.

■ Meanwhile, in a large skillet cook and stir green onions and red or green pepper in hot margarine or butter over medium-high heat for 2 minutes. Add mushrooms; cook and stir for 2 minutes more, or till vegetables are tender. Stir in half-and-half or whipping cream and heat through, but do not boil.

■ Pour mushroom-cream mixture over pasta and toss to coat pasta. Add Parmesan cheese and toss. Transfer to a warm serving dish. Sprinkle with pepper. Serve immediately.

Makes 6 side-dish servings

Per serving: 277 calories, 9 g protein, 33 g carbohydrate, 12 g total fat (5 g saturated), 18 mg cholesterol, 170 mg sodium, 225 mg potassium

INGREDIENTS

4	OUNCES DRIED *OR* 8 OUNCES FRESH PLAIN FETTUCCINE
4	OUNCES DRIED *OR* 8 OUNCES FRESH SPINACH FETTUCCINE
1/4	CUP SLICED GREEN ONIONS
1/2	CUP FINELY CHOPPED RED *OR* GREEN SWEET PEPPER
3	TABLESPOONS MARGARINE *OR* BUTTER
6	OUNCES FRESH SHIITAKE MUSHROOMS, SLICED (3 CUPS)
1	CUP HALF-AND-HALF *OR* WHIPPING CREAM
1/4	CUP GRATED PARMESAN CHEESE
	PEPPER

Preparation Time: 15 minutes
Cooking Time: 8 to 10 minutes

STEPS AT A GLANCE	Page
MAKING PASTA	8–14
CUTTING RIBBON PASTA	28
PREPARING SAUCE INGREDIENTS	16

41

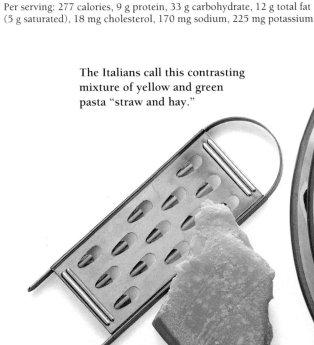

The Italians call this contrasting mixture of yellow and green pasta "straw and hay."

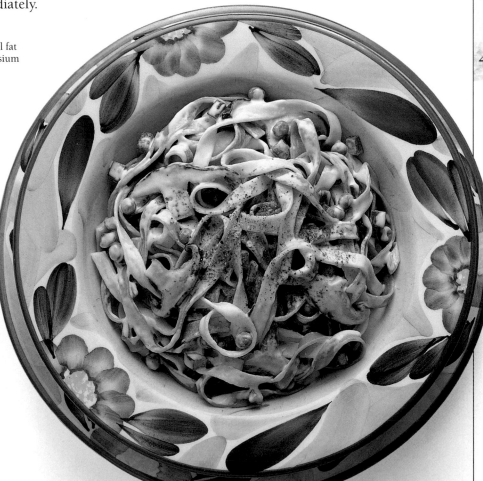

Spaghetti with Creamy Clam Sauce

Preparation Time: 20 minutes
Cooking Time: 8 to 12 minutes

INGREDIENTS

8	OUNCES DRIED SPAGHETTI *OR* LINGUINE *OR* 1 POUND FRESH LINGUINE *OR* OTHER RIBBON PASTA

SAUCE

2	6-1/2-OUNCE CANS MINCED CLAMS
	HALF-AND-HALF, LIGHT CREAM, *OR* MILK
1/2	CUP CHOPPED ONION
2	CLOVES GARLIC, MINCED
2	TABLESPOONS MARGARINE *OR* BUTTER
1/4	CUP ALL-PURPOSE FLOUR
1/2	TEASPOON DRIED BASIL *OR* OREGANO, CRUSHED
1/4	TEASPOON SALT
1/4	TEASPOON PEPPER
1/4	CUP SNIPPED FRESH PARSLEY
1/4	CUP DRY WHITE WINE
1/4	CUP GRATED PARMESAN CHEESE

42

*T*his creamy version of the ever-popular pasta with clam sauce cooks in minutes. If small cans of minced clams are pantry staples, you can prepare an enticing meal with very little notice. Serve with a green salad and crusty bread to soak up the sauce.

■ In a large saucepan or pasta pot bring 3 quarts water to boiling. Add pasta. Reduce heat slightly. Boil, uncovered, for 8 to 12 minutes for dried pasta or 1½ to 2 minutes for fresh, or till al dente, stirring occasionally. (Or, cook according to package directions.) Immediately drain.

■ Meanwhile, drain clams, reserving liquid. Add enough half-and-half, light cream, or milk to the reserved liquid to make 1¾ cups.

■ For sauce, in a medium saucepan cook the onion and garlic in hot margarine or butter for about 5 minutes, or till onion is tender but not brown. Stir in the flour, basil or oregano, salt, and pepper. Add the cream mixture all at once. Cook and stir till thickened and bubbly. Cook and stir for 1 minute more. Stir in the parsley, wine, and clams. Heat through.

■ Serve sauce over hot pasta. Sprinkle with Parmesan cheese. Serve immediately.

Makes 4 main-dish servings

Per serving: 551 calories, 21 g protein, 59 g carbohydrate, 25 g total fat (12 g saturated), 115 mg cholesterol, 401 mg sodium, 367 mg potassium

Sprinkle this seafood sauce with Parmesan cheese just before serving. It's always a good idea to grate a little extra to pass at the table.

Turkey Tetrazzini

Preparation Time: 25 minutes
Baking Time: 20 minutes

INGREDIENTS

6	OUNCES DRIED SPAGHETTI, VERMICELLI, *OR* CAPELLINI *OR* 12 OUNCES FRESH LINGUINE *OR* OTHER RIBBON PASTA
1	OUNCE DRIED TOMATOES (NOT OIL-PACKED) (8 HALVES)
1-1/2	CUPS STEMMED AND SLICED FRESH SHIITAKE MUSHROOMS *OR* REGULAR MUSHROOMS
3	TABLESPOONS MARGARINE *OR* BUTTER
1/4	CUP ALL-PURPOSE FLOUR
1/8	TEASPOON GROUND NUTMEG
1-1/2	CUPS HALF-AND-HALF, LIGHT CREAM, *OR* MILK
1	CUP CHICKEN BROTH
2-1/2	CUPS CHOPPED COOKED TURKEY *OR* CHICKEN
2	TABLESPOONS DRY SHERRY
1/4	CUP GRATED PARMESAN CHEESE
1/4	CUP SLICED ALMONDS

Use leftover cooked turkey or chicken for a pasta dish with all the flavors of an elegant pot pie.

43

A ccording to most accounts, the opera singer Luisa Tetrazzini inspired the original version of this poultry-based dish almost a century ago.

■ In a large saucepan or pasta pot bring 3 quarts water to boiling. Add pasta. Reduce heat slightly. Boil, uncovered, 10 to 12 minutes for spaghetti and 5 to 7 minutes for vermicelli or capellini, or 1½ to 2 minutes for fresh pasta, or till al dente, stirring occasionally. (Or, cook according to package directions.) Immediately drain.

■ Place dried tomatoes in a small bowl. Add enough hot water to cover; soak for 10 to 15 minutes, or till softened. Drain and pat dry. Chop tomatoes; set aside.

■ Meanwhile, in a large saucepan cook mushrooms in melted margarine or butter till tender. Stir in flour and nutmeg. Add half-and-half, light cream, or milk and chicken broth all at once. Cook and stir till thickened and bubbly. Stir in turkey or chicken, sherry, and chopped tomatoes. Add cooked pasta; toss to coat.

■ Transfer to a 2-quart rectangular baking dish. Sprinkle with Parmesan cheese and almonds. Bake in a preheated 350° oven for 20 minutes, or till heated through. Serve immediately.
Makes 6 main-dish servings

STEPS AT A GLANCE	Page
COOKING PASTA	12

Per serving: 462 calories, 29 g protein, 37 g carbohydrate, 22 g total fat (7 g saturated), 79 mg cholesterol, 481 mg sodium, 576 mg potassium

Pasta with Turkey & Tomatoes in Cream

Smoked turkey adds a dusky flavor to
an elegant pasta sauce featuring both
fresh and dried tomatoes.

Preparation Time: 20 minutes
Cooking Time: 20 minutes

INGREDIENTS

2	POUNDS RIPE PLUM TOMATOES *OR* TWO 14-1/2-OUNCE CANS WHOLE ITALIAN-STYLE TOMATOES, CUT UP
2	CLOVES GARLIC, MINCED
1/2	TEASPOON SUGAR
1/4	TEASPOON SALT
1/8	TEASPOON PEPPER
1/2	CUP WHIPPING CREAM
12	OUNCES FULLY COOKED SMOKED TURKEY BREAST, CUT INTO 2X1/4-INCH STRIPS
1/4	CUP DRAINED OIL-PACKED DRIED TOMATOES, SNIPPED
2	TABLESPOONS SNIPPED FRESH PARSLEY
8	OUNCES FUSILLI, LINGUINE, *OR* OTHER DRIED RIBBON PASTA *OR* 1 POUND FRESH LINGUINE *OR* FETTUCCINE
1/4	CUP GRATED PARMESAN CHEESE (OPTIONAL)

*G*rind fresh pepper over the top of this savory pasta to give it a boost in flavor and in appearance. Garnish with Italian parsley.

STEPS AT A GLANCE	Page
MAKING PASTA	8–14
CUTTING RIBBON PASTA	28
PREPARING SAUCE INGREDIENTS	16

■ Peel and chop fresh plum tomatoes, if using. In a large skillet heat oil over medium heat. Add fresh or undrained canned tomatoes, garlic, sugar, salt, and pepper. Bring to boiling; reduce heat. Boil gently, uncovered, for 15 minutes or till thickened, stirring occasionally. Gradually add the cream to the tomato mixture, stirring constantly. Add the turkey and dried tomatoes; heat through. Remove from heat; stir in parsley.

■ Meanwhile, in a large saucepan or pasta pot bring 3 quarts water to boiling. Add pasta. Reduce heat slightly. Boil, uncovered, 15 minutes for dried fusilli and 8 to 10 minutes for dried linguine, or 1½ to 2 minutes for fresh pasta, or till al dente, stirring occasionally. (Or, cook according to package directions.) Immediately drain.

■ Serve sauce over pasta. If desired, sprinkle with Parmesan cheese. Serve immediately.
Makes 4 main-dish servings

Per serving: 493 calories, 29 g protein, 63 g carbohydrate, 15 g total fat (8 g saturated), 77 mg cholesterol, 1,045 mg sodium, 1,076 mg potassium

Toasted Vermicelli with Fresh Salsa

*T*o give the sauce even more of a Spanish flavor, use 1 cup of clam juice and 1 cup of chicken broth, instead of 2 cups of chicken broth. This makes a tasty companion for grilled fish.

■ In a large skillet cook pasta, onion, and garlic in hot oil for 5 minutes, or till pasta is golden and onion is tender, stirring constantly. Gently stir in 2 tomatoes, the chicken broth, jalapeño peppers, oregano, cumin, and salt. Bring to boiling; reduce heat. Simmer, uncovered, for about 8 minutes, or till pasta is al dente. Stir in cilantro. Transfer to a serving dish. If desired, garnish with chopped tomatoes.

Makes 6 side-dish servings

Per serving: 166 calories, 6 g protein, 23 g carbohydrate, 6 g total fat (1 g saturated), 0 mg cholesterol, 353 mg sodium, 239 mg potassium

Preparation Time: 25 minutes
Cooking Time: 15 minutes

INGREDIENTS

5	OUNCES DRIED VERMICELLI *OR* CAPELLINI, BROKEN INTO 1/2-INCH PIECES
1/2	CUP CHOPPED ONION
1	CLOVE GARLIC, THINLY SLICED
2	TABLESPOONS OLIVE OIL *OR* COOKING OIL
2	TOMATOES, PEELED, SEEDED, AND CHOPPED
2	CUPS CHICKEN BROTH
3	FRESH JALAPEÑO PEPPERS, SEEDED AND THINLY SLICED
1/2	TEASPOON DRIED OREGANO, CRUSHED
1/4	TEASPOON GROUND CUMIN
1/4	TEASPOON SALT
2	TABLESPOONS SNIPPED FRESH CILANTRO
	CHOPPED FRESH TOMATOES (OPTIONAL)

In this unusual preparation, the vermicelli is first sautéed in oil, then cooked with the rest of the sauce.

Spaghetti & Meatballs

INGREDIENTS

CLASSIC TOMATO SAUCE (PAGE 18)

1 BEATEN EGG

3/4 CUP SOFT BREAD CRUMBS (1 SLICE)

1/4 CUP FINELY CHOPPED ONION

2 TABLESPOONS FINELY CHOPPED GREEN SWEET PEPPER

1/4 TEASPOON SALT

1/4 TEASPOON DRIED OREGANO, CRUSHED

1 POUND GROUND BEEF OR BULK PORK SAUSAGE

1 TABLESPOON COOKING OIL

8 OUNCES DRIED SPAGHETTI OR LINGUINE OR 1 POUND FRESH LINGUINE OR OTHER RIBBON PASTA

Preparation Time: 1 hour (includes sauce)
Cooking Time: 21 to 27 minutes

STEPS AT A GLANCE	Page
MAKING PASTA	8–14
CUTTING RIBBON PASTA	28
MAKING TOMATO SAUCE	18

*I*f you prefer not to brown the meatballs in a skillet, you can bake them in a preheated 375° oven for about 20 minutes, or till no pink remains. To make soft bread crumbs, shred the bread with a fork or process briefly in a blender or food processor.

■ Prepare classic tomato sauce as directed; keep warm.

■ In a large mixing bowl combine egg, bread crumbs, onion, green pepper, salt, and oregano. Add ground beef or sausage; mix well. Shape into thirty 1-inch meatballs. In a large skillet heat the oil and cook the meatballs, in 2 batches, for 8 to 10 minutes, or till no pink remains. Drain well. Add meatballs to the warm sauce. Cook, uncovered, for 5 minutes to heat through and blend flavors, stirring occasionally. Keep warm.

■ In a large saucepan or pasta pot bring 3 quarts water to boiling. Add pasta. Reduce heat slightly. Boil, uncovered, 8 to 12 minutes for dried pasta or 1½ to 2 minutes for fresh, or till al dente, stirring occasionally. (Or, cook according to package directions.) Immediately drain.

■ Serve sauce and meatballs over hot pasta.

Makes 4 to 6 main-dish servings

Per serving: 681 calories, 34 g protein, 73 g carbohydrate, 29 g total fat (8 g saturated), 123 mg cholesterol, 564 mg sodium, 1,372 mg potassium

46

Everyone's favorite pasta dish: flavorful meatballs in a simple tomato sauce on a bed of spaghetti. Sprinkle with Parmesan if desired.

Linguine with Spicy Chili Sauce & Beans

INGREDIENTS

8	OUNCES DRIED LINGUINE *OR* SPAGHETTI *OR* 1 POUND FRESH LINGUINE *OR* OTHER RIBBON PASTA

MEAT SAUCE

1	POUND RIPE PLUM TOMATOES *OR* ONE 16-OUNCE CAN TOMATOES, CUT UP
1	POUND LEAN GROUND CHICKEN, TURKEY, *OR* BEEF
1/2	CUP CHOPPED ONION
1	CLOVE GARLIC, MINCED
1	8-OUNCE CAN TOMATO SAUCE
1/4	CUP CHICKEN BROTH
1	TABLESPOON RED WINE VINEGAR
1	TABLESPOON CHILI POWDER
1/2	TEASPOON GROUND ALLSPICE
1/4	TEASPOON GROUND CINNAMON
1/4	TEASPOON SALT
1/8	TEASPOON GROUND RED PEPPER (OPTIONAL)

TOPPINGS

1	16-OUNCE CAN CANNELLINI BEANS
1/4	CUP THINLY SLICED GREEN ONIONS
1/2	CUP SHREDDED CHEDDAR CHEESE *OR* 1/4 CUP GRATED PARMESAN CHEESE

Preparation Time: 30 minutes
Cooking Time: 20 to 25 minutes

47

*I*f you ordered this dish in Cincinnati, it would be called "five-way" chili because it has it all: pasta, chili, cheese, onions, and beans.

■ In a large saucepan or pasta pot bring 3 quarts water to boiling. Add pasta. Reduce heat slightly. Boil, uncovered, for 8 to 12 minutes for dried pasta or 1½ to 2 minutes for fresh, or till al dente, stirring occasionally. (Or, cook according to package directions.) Immediately drain.

■ Meanwhile, peel, seed, and chop fresh plum tomatoes, if using. In a large skillet cook ground chicken, turkey, or beef, onion, and garlic for 5 minutes, or till meat is brown and onion is tender. Drain off fat. Stir in fresh or undrained canned tomatoes, tomato sauce, chicken broth, vinegar, chili powder, allspice, cinnamon, salt, and, if desired, red pepper. Bring to boiling; reduce heat. Simmer, uncovered, for 15 to 20 minutes, or to desired consistency, stirring occasionally.

■ To serve, heat cannellini beans in a small saucepan; drain. Top hot cooked pasta with meat sauce, beans, green onions, and cheddar or Parmesan cheese. Serve immediately.

Makes 4 to 6 main-dish servings

Per serving: 530 calories, 36 g protein, 74 g carbohydrate, 13 g total fat (5 g saturated), 69 mg cholesterol, 866 mg sodium, 993 mg potassium

This surprising rendition of pasta and meat sauce features the bold flavors of classic chili.

STEPS AT A GLANCE	Page
MAKING PASTA	8–14
CUTTING RIBBON PASTA	28
PREPARING SAUCE INGREDIENTS	16
SIMMERING SAUCE	18

Stir-fried Vegetables with Buckwheat Noodles

Preparation Time: 30 minutes
Cooking Time: 16 to 17 minutes

INGREDIENTS

4	OUNCES DRIED BUCKWHEAT NOODLES (SOBA), CHINESE EGG NOODLES, OR FINE EGG NOODLES

SAUCE

1/2	CUP CHICKEN BROTH
1	TABLESPOON CORNSTARCH
1	TABLESPOON SOY SAUCE
2	TEASPOONS TOASTED SESAME OIL

VEGETABLES

1	TABLESPOON COOKING OIL
1	10-1/2-OUNCE PACKAGE EXTRA-FIRM TOFU, DRAINED AND CUT INTO THIN STRIPS
2	TEASPOONS GRATED FRESH GINGERROOT
2	CLOVES GARLIC, CUT INTO SLIVERS (1 TEASPOON)
1	RED OR YELLOW SWEET PEPPER, CUT INTO THIN STRIPS
1	CUP FRESH PEA PODS (SNOW PEAS)
1	CUP SLICED YELLOW SUMMER SQUASH OR ZUCCHINI
3	GREEN ONIONS, BIAS-SLICED INTO 1-INCH PIECES

Soba noodles, made from buckwheat, are a favorite in Japan and are enjoyed either hot or cold.

*P*asta shows off its wonderful versatility: It's not just for meals with an Italian accent, as you'll see when you taste this Asian-style dish.

■ In a large saucepan or pasta pot bring 3 quarts water to boiling. Add buckwheat noodles or Chinese egg noodles. Reduce heat slightly. Boil, uncovered, 10 minutes for buckwheat noodles or 4 to 6 minutes for Chinese egg noodles, or till al dente, stirring occasionally. (Or, cook according to package directions.) Immediately drain.

■ Meanwhile, for sauce, in a small mixing bowl stir together chicken broth, cornstarch, soy sauce, and sesame oil; set aside.

■ For vegetables, in a large skillet heat cooking oil over medium-high heat. Add tofu, gingerroot, and garlic. Cook for 2 minutes, or till tofu is heated through, turning tofu once. Remove from skillet. Add red or yellow sweet pepper, yellow summer squash or zucchini, and green onions to skillet. Stir-fry for 2 to 3 minutes, or till crisp-tender. Push vegetables to sides of skillet. Stir sauce and add to center of skillet. Cook and stir till thickened and bubbly. Return tofu and noodles to skillet. Stir all ingredients together to coat with sauce; heat through and serve immediately.

Makes 4 main-dish servings

Per serving: 231 calories, 13 g protein, 31 g carbohydrate, 8 g total fat (1 g saturated), 0 mg cholesterol, 602 mg sodium, 380 mg potassium

48

Szechwan Chicken & Pasta

Preparation Time: 25 minutes
Cooking Time: 11 to 13 minutes

INGREDIENTS

1	POUND BONELESS, SKINLESS CHICKEN BREAST HALVES
2	CUPS FRESH PEA PODS (SNOW PEAS) OR ONE 6-OUNCE PACKAGE FROZEN PEA PODS, THAWED
1/4	CUP SOY SAUCE
2	TABLESPOONS RICE VINEGAR OR WHITE WINE VINEGAR
1	TEASPOON CHILI OIL
1/4	TO 1/2 TEASPOON CRUSHED RED PEPPER
5	OUNCES DRIED CHINESE EGG NOODLES OR 8 OUNCES FRESH CHINESE EGG NOODLES
1	TABLESPOON COOKING OIL
2	CLOVES GARLIC, MINCED
1	LARGE RED OR GREEN SWEET PEPPER, CUT INTO THIN STRIPS (1-1/3 CUPS)
2	GREEN ONIONS, SLICED (1/4 CUP)
1/4	CUP COARSELY CHOPPED PEANUTS

*C*hinese egg noodles are made from wheat flour, water, and egg and are shaped either round or flat. They are available fresh or dried. Many well-stocked supermarkets carry fresh noodles in the produce department along with spring-roll wrappers. You can substitute any fresh ribbon pasta for the fresh Chinese noodles, if you prefer.

■ Rinse chicken and pat dry. Cut into ¾-inch pieces. Coarsely chop the pea pods. In a small bowl stir together the soy sauce, vinegar, chili oil, and crushed red pepper. Set aside.

■ For dried noodles, in a large saucepan or pasta pot bring 3 quarts water to boiling. Add noodles. Reduce heat slightly. Boil, uncovered, 4 to 6 minutes, or till tender, stirring occasionally. (Prepare fresh noodles according to package directions.) Drain.

■ Pour cooking oil into a wok or large skillet. (Add more oil as necessary during cooking). Preheat over medium-high heat. Stir-fry the garlic in hot oil for 15 seconds. Add the pea pods, red or green pepper, and green onions; stir-fry for 1 to 2 minutes, or till crisp-tender. Remove the vegetables from the wok.

■ Add half of the chicken to the hot wok. Stir-fry for 2 to 3 minutes, or till no pink remains. Remove the chicken from the wok. Repeat with remaining chicken. Return all chicken to the wok. Add the soy sauce mixture to the wok. Add the cooked vegetables and noodles. Stir ingredients together to coat with soy sauce mixture. Cook and stir about 1 minute more, or till heated through. Sprinkle with peanuts. Serve immediately.

Makes 5 main-dish servings

Per serving: 369 calories, 27 g protein, 39 g carbohydrate, 12 g total fat (2 g saturated), 87 mg cholesterol, 910 mg sodium, 407 mg potassium

49

This pasta meal-in-a-bowl is full of healthy vegetables, low-fat chicken, and a tangy mixture of soy sauce, chili oil, and rice vinegar.

Filipino-Style Noodles

INGREDIENTS

1/2	CUP CHOPPED ONION
2	CLOVES GARLIC, MINCED
2	TABLESPOONS COOKING OIL
1	CUP THINLY BIAS-SLICED CARROTS
1	SMALL ZUCCHINI, CUT INTO SHORT, THIN STRIPS
1	CUP SHREDDED CABBAGE
1	CUP CHICKEN BROTH
2	TABLESPOONS SOY SAUCE
3/4	CUP COOKED PORK, SLICED INTO THIN STRIPS
3/4	CUP COOKED SHRIMP, CHOPPED
8	OUNCES PANCIT CANTON NOODLES OR DRIED CHINESE EGG NOODLES
1/4	CUP THINLY SLICED GREEN ONIONS (OPTIONAL)

Preparation Time: 25 minutes
Cooking Time: 12 minutes

STEPS AT A GLANCE	Page
PREPARING SAUCE INGREDIENTS	16

*P*ancit canton noodles are a favorite in the Philippines, where pancit means "noodle." Because they are pre-cooked and sold dried, they need only be added to boiling liquid for a brief time before they are tender.

■ In a 12-inch skillet cook onion and garlic in hot oil for 5 minutes, or till tender but not brown. Add carrots, zucchini, cabbage, chicken broth, and soy sauce; mix well. Bring to boiling; reduce heat. Cover and simmer for 5 minutes, or till carrots are crisp-tender. Stir in pork and shrimp.

■ Break noodles apart and stir into cooked mixture. (If necessary, add additional chicken broth to cook noodles.) Cover and cook over low heat about 2 minutes for pancit canton noodles and 4 to 6 minutes for egg noodles, or till noodles are tender and liquid is absorbed. Stir mixture gently and transfer to a serving dish. If desired, sprinkle with green onions.

Makes 4 main-dish servings

Per serving: 407 calories, 22 g protein, 51 g carbohydrate, 12 g total fat (3 g saturated), 79 mg cholesterol, 1,861 mg sodium, 553 mg potassium

50

If you like egg rolls, this stir-fry is for you: It contains all the same ingredients served over long wheat noodles.

Shaped Pasta

Steps for Making Shaped Pasta

BASIC TOOLS FOR MAKING SHAPED PASTA

Cut basic rectangles and circles for shaping from pasta dough with a fluted pastry wheel and a ruler, or a round biscuit cutter.

BISCUIT CUTTER

CUTTING BOARD

FLUTED PASTRY
WHEEL

RULER

52

ONLY A VERY FEW of the hundreds of charming pasta shapes that are turned out so effortlessly in the factory can be formed by hand.

Farfalle, which to some resemble little butterflies and to others bow ties, may be the easiest to do. They begin as small rectangles of dough cut from a freshly rolled sheet. If you prefer them with a decoratively pinked edge, use a fluted pastry wheel to cut them. Otherwise, any sharp knife or a straight-edge pizza cutter will work well.

Tripolini are also described as bow ties, but rather than having crisp, straight edges and sharp, angular corners, they are rounded like the bow ties worn by circus clowns. They are formed in the same way as farfalle, but begin as circles rather than rectangles.

Orecchiette are thin cups said to have originated in Apulia, an Italian region that makes up the heel of Italy's boot. This is a wonderful pasta for sauces because it not only absorbs the sauce, but traps it inside the cup.

For any of these shapes, prepare Homemade Pasta dough, page 14, as directed, then follow the steps on the

opposite page. Let the shaped pasta dry partially on a flour-dusted towel or baking sheet before cooking, or dry it completely if storing in the refrigerator. Turn occasionally to expose both sides to the air.

Homemade farfalle and tripolini will cook in 2 to 3 minutes. Orecchiette are thicker and take a little more time, 6 to 7 minutes. All three are available as packaged dried pastas, too. These pastas are delicious served hot with meat and vegetable sauces. Florentine-inspired Chicken Livers over Pasta, page 66, features chicken livers and farfalle or tripolini in a creamy sauce dotted with colorful bits of red and green sweet peppers. Orecchiette with Fennel in Parmesan Cream, page 68, is an anise-flavored combination of fresh fennel and Sambuca plus mushrooms and Italian prosciutto ham. These shapes are attractive additions to cold salads as well. Warm Tomato–Feta Cheese Salad, page 115, is a refreshing summer dish that shows off farfalle — either fresh or dried.

you can also use a pizza wheel or a knife to cut the strips

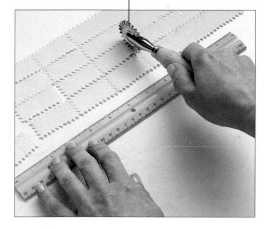

STEP 1 MAKING FARFALLE (BOW TIES)

Roll the dough ¹⁄₁₆ inch thick and trim the sides so that they are straight and even. Using a fluted pastry wheel, cut the dough into 1-inch-wide strips. Then cut crosswise every 2 inches to form 2x1-inch rectangles.

if the pasta is too dry to hold the pinch, dab a little water in the center

STEP 2 SHAPING FARFALLE

To form the bow tie, pinch the center of the rectangle. To create a nice fold, first lay your index finger or little finger sideways in the center of the dough and pinch against it. Remove your finger and finish making the pinch.

save and reroll dough scraps to make more pasta

STEP 3 MAKING TRIPOLINI

Using a 1- or 1¼-inch round cutter, cut the dough into circles. Shape as for farfalle (step 2): Pinch the center of each circle to form a rounded bow tie.

53

don't flour the work surface or the dough too heavily or the log will slide instead of rolling

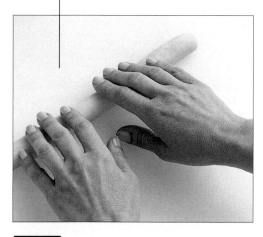

STEP 4 MAKING ORECCHIETTE

Shape 4 to 6 ounces of pasta dough into a log ½ inch in diameter. Roll with even pressure to avoid denting the dough and to keep it uniformly thick.

flour your hands as needed to keep the pasta from sticking

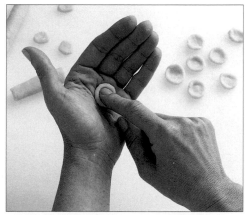

STEP 5 SHAPING ORECCHIETTE

With a sharp knife, slice the roll into ¹⁄₈-inch-thick slices. Place one slice in your palm. Shape it into a little cup by pressing the middle of the slice with your index finger. Twist your finger to broaden the cup.

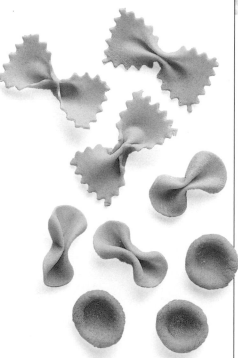

Whimsical pasta shapes like farfalle (bow ties), tripolini (rounded bow ties), and orecchiette ("little ears") are easily formed by hand.

Dried Shaped Pasta

NOWHERE IS THE playful side of the Italian character better illustrated than in the myriad shapes of dried pasta offered by commercial manufacturers. There are literally hundreds. Where else but in Italy would you eat food that looks like little radiators (radiatori) and cork-screws (fusilli), thimbles (ditali) and shells (conchiglie), bow ties (farfalle) and little ears (orecchiette), wheels (ruote) and rice or barley (orzo)! Often the same shape appears in several sizes (the smaller often ends in *ini* or *etti*, which are diminutives). For example, ditali are tubes about ½ inch long; ditalini are shorter. The same shape may be called one thing in one region and another else-where. One name can even be applied to more than one shape! Confusing, yes. A problem, not at all. Most shapes are interchangeable.

Dried shaped pasta complements sauces with large pieces of vegetables, similar in size to the pasta. Shells, spirals, and rigatoni go with meaty sauces because their indentations trap bits of ingredients. Small shells, elbow macaroni, and tubular ditali are good in soups.

to use with a sauce, cook shaped pasta in boiling water as shown on pages 12 and 13

STEP 1 ADDING PASTA TO BOILING BROTH
Bring a large pot of flavorful broth to a rolling boil. Add pasta to the broth gradually, so that it keeps boiling. The pasta will absorb much of the cooking liquid, so be sure to use a generous amount of broth.

Dried pasta is available in a delightful array of shapes, including elbows, bow ties, wheels, tubes, and shells.

54

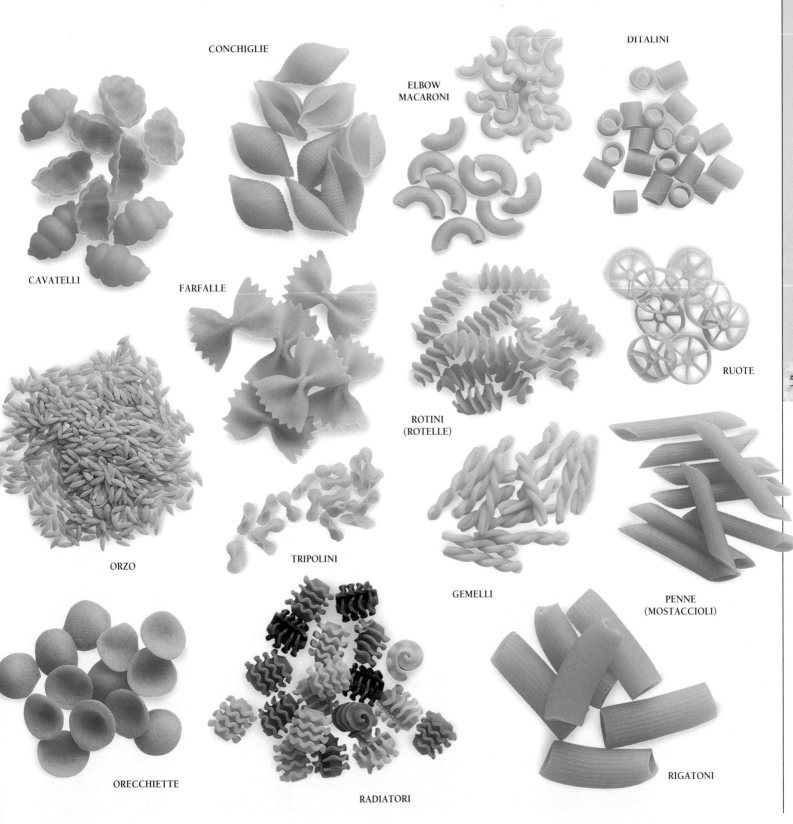

CONCHIGLIE

ELBOW
MACARONI

DITALINI

CAVATELLI

FARFALLE

ROTINI
(ROTELLE)

RUOTE

ORZO

TRIPOLINI

GEMELLI

PENNE
(MOSTACCIOLI)

ORECCHIETTE

RADIATORI

RIGATONI

Pasta & Shrimp in Asparagus Sauce

Preparation Time: 30 minutes
Cooking Time: 15 minutes

INGREDIENTS

12	OUNCES FRESH *OR* FROZEN SHRIMP, PEELED AND DEVEINED
1-1/2	POUNDS FRESH ASPARAGUS SPEARS
8	OUNCES GEMELLI, ROTINI, *OR* OTHER DRIED SHAPED PASTA
1	CUP CHICKEN BROTH
1/4	CUP DAIRY SOUR CREAM
2	TABLESPOONS ALL-PURPOSE FLOUR
1/4	TEASPOON SALT
1/8	TEASPOON WHITE PEPPER
1	TABLESPOON LEMON JUICE

*W*hen setting aside asparagus pieces before puréeing, choose only the tips, which are usually the most tender part of the stalk and the most attractive.

■ Thaw shrimp, if frozen. Snap off and discard woody asparagus bases. Cut spears into 1½-inch pieces. Cook, covered, in a small amount of boiling water for 6 to 8 minutes, or till crisp-tender. Drain, reserving ¼ cup of the cooking liquid. Set aside 1 cup of the asparagus pieces; keep warm. In a blender container or food processor bowl, purée remaining asparagus with the reserved cooking liquid till nearly smooth.

■ Meanwhile, in a large saucepan or pasta pot bring 3 quarts water to boiling. Add pasta. Reduce heat slightly. Boil, uncovered, for 8 to 10 minutes. Add shrimp to boiling pasta during the last 3 minutes of cooking. Cook till pasta is al dente and shrimp turn pink, stirring occasionally (Or, cook according to package directions, adding shrimp the last 3 minutes.) Immediately drain. Return pasta and shrimp to warm pan; add asparagus pieces.

■ In a medium saucepan stir together chicken broth, sour cream, flour, salt, and pepper. Add asparagus purée and lemon juice. Cook and stir over medium heat till thickened and bubbly. Cook and stir for 1 minute more. Pour sauce over hot pasta mixture and toss to coat. Serve immediately.

Makes 4 main-dish servings

Per serving: 356 calories, 24 g protein, 53 g carbohydrate, 5 g total fat (2 g saturated), 116 mg cholesterol, 465 mg sodium, 497 mg potassium

STEPS AT A GLANCE	Page
PEELING SHRIMP	36
COOKING PASTA	12
MAKING ASPARAGUS SAUCE	56

56

STEPS FOR MAKING ASPARAGUS SAUCE

STEP 1 PREPARING ASPARAGUS
Hold the asparagus stalk in both hands and press with your thumbs toward the thicker end. Snap off the woody base and discard.

STEP 2 MAKING PURÉE
Cook asparagus pieces in boiling water until crisp-tender. Blend all but 1 cup with the reserved cooking water in a blender or food processor to a chunky purée.

When asparagus makes its long-awaited appearance in the spring, use the delicate vegetable to make this elegant main course.

Artichokes and lamb pair in a Greek-
inspired sauce served over tiny pasta
that resembles grains of barley.

58

Artichokes, Lamb & Orzo Avgolemono

INGREDIENTS

2	TABLESPOONS OLIVE OIL OR COOKING OIL
1	POUND BONELESS LEAN LAMB, CUT INTO 3/4-INCH CUBES
1	CUP CHOPPED ONION
1	GARLIC CLOVE, MINCED
3/4	CUP WHITE WINE OR CHICKEN BROTH
1-1/2	TEASPOONS SNIPPED FRESH OREGANO OR 1/2 TEASPOON DRIED OREGANO, CRUSHED
1	TEASPOON FINELY SHREDDED LEMON PEEL
1/4	TEASPOON SALT
1/4	TEASPOON PEPPER
6	FRESH MEDIUM ARTICHOKES, TRIMMED, HALVED, AND BLANCHED, OR ONE 9-OUNCE PACKAGE FROZEN ARTICHOKE HEARTS
8	OUNCES ORZO (1-1/3 CUPS)
1	BEATEN EGG
2	TABLESPOONS LEMON JUICE
1	TABLESPOON CORNSTARCH
1/2	CUP WARM CHICKEN BROTH
2	TABLESPOONS SNIPPED FRESH PARSLEY (OPTIONAL)

*A*vgolemono, a Greek sauce made with lemon juice and egg, is the base for this Mediterranean-style lamb and artichoke topping for orzo pasta. Try leg of lamb, sirloin, or shoulder for lean cuts of lamb.

■ In a Dutch oven or large skillet heat the oil and brown half of the lamb; remove meat. Brown remaining meat with onion and garlic till onion is tender. Drain fat from all of the meat. Return all the meat to pan. Stir in ¾ cup wine or chicken broth, oregano, lemon peel, salt, and pepper. Bring to boiling; reduce heat. Cover; simmer for 20 minutes. Add fresh or frozen artichokes and simmer 10 minutes more, or till tender.

■ Meanwhile, in a large saucepan or pasta pot bring 3 quarts water to boiling. Add pasta. Reduce heat slightly. Boil, uncovered, for 5 to 8 minutes, or till al dente, stirring occasionally. (Or, cook according to package directions.) Immediately drain. Return to warm pan; keep warm.

■ In a small mixing bowl combine egg, lemon juice, cornstarch, and ½ cup warm chicken broth. Pour egg mixture into the lamb-artichoke mixture. Cook and stir over medium heat for 1 minute, or till thickened and bubbly. Cook and stir for 2 minutes more. Serve lamb mixture over hot cooked pasta. If desired, garnish with parsley.

Makes 4 main-dish servings

Per serving: 525 calories, 31 g protein, 61 g carbohydrate, 15 g total fat (3 g saturated), 111 mg cholesterol, 356 mg sodium, 661 mg potassium

Preparation Time: 20 minutes
Cooking Time: 45 minutes

STEPS AT A GLANCE	Page
PREPARING ARTICHOKES	59
PREPARING SAUCE INGREDIENTS	16
COOKING PASTA	12

59

STEPS FOR PREPARING ARTICHOKES

STEP 1 TRIMMING ARTICHOKES

Trim stem flush with bottom. Break off tough outer leaves until only soft ones with a tinge of yellow remain.

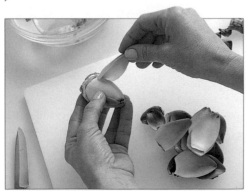

STEP 2 REMOVING CHOKES

Trim leaves to about 1 inch long. Cut artichoke in half to expose the choke. Scoop out the hairy choke with a tiny spoon or a melon baller and discard.

STEP 3 ADDING HEARTS TO WATER

Fill a bowl with water and squeeze some lemon juice into it, then drop in the lemon slices. To prevent browning, float trimmed pieces in acidulated water until needed.

Stuffed Peppers with Orzo

Preparation Time: 20 minutes
Baking Time: 15 minutes

INGREDIENTS

2	LARGE RED, YELLOW, *AND/OR* GREEN SWEET PEPPERS
12	OUNCES GROUND LAMB, TURKEY, *OR* PORK
1/3	CUP CHOPPED ONION
1	8-OUNCE CAN STEWED TOMATOES
1/3	CUP ORZO
1	TABLESPOON SNIPPED FRESH MINT, BASIL, *OR* OREGANO, *OR* 1/2 TEASPOON DRIED MINT, BASIL, *OR* OREGANO, CRUSHED
1/2	TEASPOON GROUND ALLSPICE
1/2	CUP WATER
1/4	TEASPOON SALT
1/4	TEASPOON PEPPER
1/2	CUP SHREDDED KASSERI *OR* GRATED PARMESAN CHEESE

*O*rzo *is a barley-shaped pasta frequently used in recipes as a substitute for rice. Here it cooks in the stuffing mixture, saving the step of cooking the pasta separately.*

■ Halve peppers lengthwise, removing stem ends, seeds, and membranes. Immerse peppers in boiling water for 3 minutes. Remove and sprinkle insides with salt. Invert peppers on paper towels to drain well.

■ In a skillet cook lamb, turkey, or pork and onion for 5 minutes, or till meat is brown and onion is tender. Drain fat. Stir in stewed tomatoes, uncooked pasta, mint, basil, or oregano, allspice, water, salt, and pepper. Bring to boiling; reduce heat. Cover and simmer for 7 to 8 minutes, or till pasta is al dente. Stir in ¼ cup of the kasseri or Parmesan cheese. Fill peppers with meat mixture.

■ Place in a 2-quart square baking dish along with any remaining meat mixture. Bake in a preheated 375° oven for about 15 minutes, or till heated through. Sprinkle with remaining cheese. Let stand for 1 to 2 minutes before serving.

Makes 4 main-dish servings

Per serving: 327 calories, 24 g protein, 22 g carbohydrate, 16 g total fat (8 g saturated), 68 mg cholesterol, 458 mg sodium, 509 mg potassium

STEPS FOR STUFFING PEPPERS

STEP 1 DRAINING PEPPERS

Drop stemmed and seeded pepper halves in boiling water for several minutes to soften. Remove from the water with tongs, sprinkle the insides with salt, and drain on paper towels, cut-side down.

STEP 2 STUFFING PEPPERS

Prepare the meat mixture, add the orzo, and cook until tender. Add cheese. Turn the peppers cut-side up. Spoon one fourth of the filling into each pepper half. Transfer to a baking dish.

Stuff colorful peppers with a Middle
Eastern filling of spice-scented
ground lamb and orzo instead
of the usual rice.

The sunny flavors and colors of
the Mediterranean are captured
in this sauce.

Pasta with Tapenade

Preparation Time: 20 minutes
Cooking Time: 12 to 14 minutes

INGREDIENTS

8	OUNCES CAVATELLI, CONCHIGLIE, *OR* OTHER DRIED SHAPED PASTA
1/2	OF A FENNEL BULB *OR* 1/2 CUP CELERY, BIAS-SLICED 1/4 INCH THICK
1/2	OF A RED SWEET PEPPER, CUT INTO THIN BITE-SIZE STRIPS
1/2	OF A YELLOW SWEET PEPPER, CUT INTO THIN BITE-SIZE STRIPS
1/2	CUP PITTED BLACK GREEK OLIVES, NIÇOISE OLIVES, *OR* PITTED RIPE OLIVES
1	3 1/2-OUNCE CAN TUNA (WATER PACK), DRAINED
1	TABLESPOON CAPERS, DRAINED
1/2	TEASPOON DRIED OREGANO *OR* THYME, CRUSHED
1	TEASPOON ANCHOVY PASTE (OPTIONAL)
1	CLOVE GARLIC
1	TABLESPOON OLIVE OIL *OR* COOKING OIL
1	TO 2 TEASPOONS LEMON JUICE
2	TABLESPOONS SNIPPED FRESH PARSLEY

*T*apenade, a purée of olives, capers, and anchovies, is generally offered as an appetizer served with bread, but it also makes a splendid main course when tossed with hot pasta.

■ In a large saucepan or pasta pot bring 3 quarts water to boiling. Add pasta. Reduce heat slightly. Boil, uncovered, for 12 to 14 minutes, or till pasta is al dente, stirring occasionally. Add fennel and red and yellow sweet pepper during the last 2 minutes of cooking. (Or, cook according to package directions, adding fennel and sweet pepper the last 2 minutes.) Immediately drain. Return pasta-vegetable mixture to warm pan.

■ Meanwhile, in a food processor bowl or blender container place the olives, tuna, capers, oregano or thyme, anchovy paste (if desired), garlic, and oil. Process or blend till mixture is smooth. Add lemon juice to taste. Add tuna mixture and parsley to hot cooked pasta mixture and toss to coat. Serve immediately.

Makes 4 main-dish servings

Per serving: 315 calories, 15 g protein, 49 g carbohydrate, 8 g total fat (1 g saturated), 4 mg cholesterol, 138 mg sodium, 187 mg potassium

STEPS FOR PREPARING FENNEL

STEP 1 CUTTING FENNEL

Trim away the feathery stalks just above where the bulb begins. Leave the root end on. If necessary, remove any damaged outer stalks.

STEP 2 SLICING FENNEL

Cut the trimmed bulb in half. Rinse between the layers to remove any grit. Lay one half on a cutting board, cut-side down. Cut into ¼-inch-thick slices with a sharp knife.

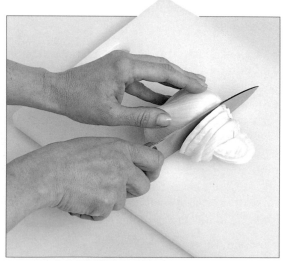

Scallops & Penne in Red Sauce

Long, narrow tubes of penne provide an attractive visual contrast to rounds of succulent scallops and bits of fresh tomato.

Preparation Time: 30 minutes
Cooking Time: 20 minutes

INGREDIENTS

12	OUNCES FRESH *OR* FROZEN SCALLOPS
8	OUNCES PENNE, RIGATONI, *OR* OTHER DRIED SHAPED PASTA
2	CLOVES GARLIC, MINCED
2	TABLESPOONS OLIVE OIL *OR* COOKING OIL
1/2	CUP DRY VERMOUTH *OR* RED WINE
2	TEASPOONS CORNSTARCH
2	POUNDS RIPE PLUM TOMATOES, PEELED, SEEDED, AND FINELY CHOPPED
1	4-OUNCE JAR DICED PIMIENTO, DRAINED
2	TABLESPOONS SNIPPED FRESH PARSLEY
2	TABLESPOONS SNIPPED FRESH BASIL
1/2	TEASPOON SALT
1/4	TEASPOON CRUSHED RED PEPPER
1/4	CUP GRATED PARMESAN CHEESE (OPTIONAL)

*W*atch the scallops carefully as they cook and remove them the second they become opaque, or they will quickly become rubbery.

■ Thaw scallops, if frozen. In a large saucepan or pasta pot bring 3 quarts water to boiling. Add pasta. Reduce heat slightly. Boil, uncovered, for 14 to 15 minutes, or till al dente, stirring occasionally. (Or, cook according to package directions.) Immediately drain.

■ Meanwhile, halve the scallops, if large. In a large skillet cook and stir the garlic in hot oil for 1 minute. Add the scallops. Cook and stir for 2 minutes more, or till scallops are opaque. Remove scallops from skillet; keep warm.

■ In the skillet stir together the vermouth or red wine and cornstarch. Stir in tomatoes, pimiento, parsley, basil, salt, and red pepper. Cook and stir till thickened and bubbly. Cook and stir for 2 minutes more. Add hot cooked pasta and scallops and toss to coat with tomato mixture. Serve immediately with Parmesan cheese, if desired.

Makes 4 main-dish servings

Per serving: 409 calories, 20 g protein, 55 g carbohydrate, 9 g total fat (1 g saturated), 25 mg cholesterol, 417 mg sodium, 651 mg potassium

STEPS AT A GLANCE	Page
PREPARING SAUCE INGREDIENTS	16
COOKING PASTA	12

64

Pesto Pasta with Vegetables

*B*ring the pesto to room temperature if you've had it stored in the refrigerator or freezer. Or, substitute purchased pesto for homemade.

■ Prepare pesto as directed. Set aside.

■ Cut potatoes into halves if very small or into bite-size pieces. Cut green beans into 2-inch pieces. In a medium saucepan cook potatoes and green beans in a small amount of boiling salted water for about 10 minutes, or till vegetables are tender. Drain well.

■ Meanwhile, in a large saucepan or pasta pot bring 3 quarts water to boiling. Add pasta. Reduce heat slightly. Boil, uncovered, for 8 to 12 minutes, or till al dente, stirring occasionally. (Or, cook according to package directions.) Immediately drain. Return pasta to warm pan. Add potatoes and green beans.

■ In a small mixing bowl stir together pesto and enough of the water to make a saucy mixture. Pour the pesto mixture and Parmesan cheese over the pasta and vegetables and toss to coat. Serve immediately.

Makes 4 side-dish servings

Per serving: 274 calories, 10 g protein, 40 g carbohydrate, 9 g total fat (2 g saturated), 7 mg cholesterol, 154 mg sodium, 471 mg potassium

INGREDIENTS

1/4	CUP PESTO (PAGE 22)
8	OUNCES WHOLE TINY NEW POTATOES
6	OUNCES GREEN BEANS
4	OUNCES RADIATORI, ROTINI, *OR* OTHER DRIED SHAPED PASTA
1	TO 2 TABLESPOONS WATER
2	TABLESPOONS GRATED PARMESAN CHEESE

Preparation Time: 35 minutes (includes pesto)
Cooking Time: 8 to 12 minutes

STEPS AT A GLANCE	Page
MAKING PESTO	22
COOKING PASTA	12

65

When you bite into crinkly radiatori, they release a burst of the sauce trapped in their deep folds.

Chicken Livers over Pasta

*I*talian cooks, particularly Florentines, adore chicken livers. One of the many good culinary uses to which they put them is this rich and hearty sauce for pasta. They're served with shaped pasta so that you can pick up a delicious morsel of liver with each bite.

■ In a large saucepan or pasta pot bring 3 quarts water to boiling. Add pasta. Reduce heat slightly. Boil, uncovered, 10 minutes for dried farfalle (5 to 6 minutes for dried tripolini) or 2 to 3 minutes for fresh, or till al dente, stirring occasionally. (Or, cook according to package directions.) Immediately drain. Return pasta to warm pan.

■ Meanwhile, in a large skillet cook chicken livers in hot margarine or butter over medium-high heat, turning as needed, for 4 to 5 minutes, or till centers are just slightly pink. Remove from skillet; keep warm. Reserve pan drippings.

■ In the same skillet cook the green onion and green and red sweet pepper in the pan drippings for 2 to 3 minutes, or till tender. Stir in flour, salt, and pepper. Add chicken broth, half-and-half, light cream, or milk, and sage. Cook and stir till thickened and bubbly. Cook and stir for 1 minute more. Pour sauce over hot cooked pasta and toss to coat. Add chicken livers; toss gently. Serve immediately.

Makes 4 main-dish servings

Per serving: 475 calories, 24 g protein, 53 g carbohydrate, 18 g total fat (7 g saturated), 359 mg cholesterol, 503 mg sodium, 290 mg potassium

Dress up chicken livers by serving them with pasta shaped like little bow ties.

Preparation Time: 25 minutes
Cooking Time: 10 minutes

INGREDIENTS

8	OUNCES DRIED *OR* 16 OUNCES FRESH FARFALLE *OR* TRIPOLINI
12	OUNCES CHICKEN LIVERS, CUT IN HALF
2	TABLESPOONS MARGARINE *OR* BUTTER
1/4	CUP SLICED GREEN ONION
1/4	CUP CHOPPED GREEN SWEET PEPPER
1/4	CUP CHOPPED RED SWEET PEPPER
1/2	CUP ALL-PURPOSE FLOUR
1/4	TEASPOON SALT
1/4	TEASPOON PEPPER
1-1/3	CUPS CHICKEN BROTH
2/3	CUP HALF-AND-HALF, LIGHT CREAM, *OR* MILK
1	TABLESPOON SNIPPED FRESH SAGE

Piselli e Pasta (Peas & Pasta)

Inspired by a Venetian classic made with peas and rice, this seasoned pasta side dish is an ideal accompaniment to any roasted fowl.

Preparation Time: 20 minutes
Cooking Time: 12 to 14 minutes

INGREDIENTS

4	OUNCES CONCHIGLIE, CAVATELLI, OR OTHER DRIED SHAPED PASTA
1	OUNCE PANCETTA OR BACON, FINELY CHOPPED
1/2	CUP THINLY SLICED GREEN ONIONS
2	TABLESPOONS MARGARINE OR BUTTER
1/2	OF A 10-OUNCE PACKAGE FROZEN SMALL PEAS (1 CUP)
1	TABLESPOON WATER
1/2	CUP MASCARPONE CHEESE
	SALT AND PEPPER (OPTIONAL)
1	TO 2 TABLESPOONS MILK (OPTIONAL)

67

*M*ascarpone is a buttery, rich and delicately flavored soft cheese from Italy. A suitable substitute is 4 ounces of cream cheese blended with 1 tablespoon of margarine or butter.

■ In a large saucepan or pasta pot bring 3 quarts water to boiling. Add pasta. Reduce heat slightly. Boil, uncovered, for 12 to 14 minutes, or till al dente, stirring occasionally. (Or, cook according to package directions.) Immediately drain.

■ Meanwhile, in a medium saucepan cook and stir pancetta (if using) and onions in hot margarine or butter for 2 minutes, or till onion is tender, but not brown. (If using bacon, omit margarine or butter and cook with onions as directed.) Add frozen peas and water to saucepan. Cover and simmer for 3 minutes. Gently stir in mascarpone cheese till melted. If desired, season to taste with salt and pepper. Add hot cooked pasta and toss to coat with cheese mixture. If mixture is too thick, add milk to thin to desired consistency. Serve immediately.

Makes 6 side-dish servings

STEPS AT A GLANCE	Page
COOKING PASTA	12

Per serving: 178 calories, 6 g protein, 19 g carbohydrate, 9 g total fat (5 g saturated), 24 mg cholesterol, 88 mg sodium, 76 mg potassium

Orecchiette with Fennel in Parmesan Cream

*T*ranslated *from the Italian,* orecchiette *means "little ears," a good description of their appearance. This is a very appealing pasta that can be made by hand (see page 53) or purchased dried. Here it pairs with a complex sauce that features exotic mushrooms and strips of Italian ham.*

■ In a large saucepan or pasta pot bring 3 quarts water to boiling. Add pasta. Reduce heat slightly. Boil, uncovered, 9 to 12 minutes for dried pasta or 2 to 3 minutes for fresh, or till al dente, stirring occasionally. (Or, cook according to package directions.) Drain.

■ Meanwhile, clean, trim, and slice the fennel bulb. Clean mushrooms; remove stems and discard. Slice mushroom caps.

■ In a large skillet cook and stir the fennel over medium-high heat in hot margarine or butter for 3 minutes. Add the mushrooms and onion. Cook and stir for 5 minutes more. Add prosciutto and parsley.

■ In a small mixing bowl combine whipping cream, Parmesan cheese, chicken broth, egg, anise liqueur or anise extract, and aniseed. Pour cream mixture into skillet. Cook and stir till cheese melts and sauce thickens slightly. Add hot cooked pasta and toss to coat pasta well. Serve immediately.

Makes 6 side-dish servings

Per serving: 298 calories, 11 g protein, 20 g carbohydrate, 19 g total fat (8 g saturated), 69 mg cholesterol, 450 mg sodium, 212 mg potassium

Preparation Time: 20 minutes
Cooking Time: 10 minutes

INGREDIENTS

4	OUNCES DRIED *OR* 8 OUNCES FRESH ORECCHIETTE
1	FENNEL BULB
3	TO 4 OUNCES FRESH CRIMINI *OR* SHIITAKE MUSHROOMS
3	TABLESPOONS MARGARINE *OR* BUTTER
1/2	CUP FINELY CHOPPED ONION
2	OUNCES PROSCIUTTO, CUT INTO THIN BITE-SIZE STRIPS
1/3	CUP SNIPPED FRESH PARSLEY
1/2	CUP WHIPPING CREAM
1/2	CUP GRATED PARMESAN CHEESE
1/4	CUP CHICKEN BROTH
1	BEATEN EGG
1	TABLESPOON SAMBUCA OR OTHER ANISE LIQUEUR *OR* 1/2 TEASPOON ANISE EXTRACT
1/2	TEASPOON ANISEED

Anise liqueur and aniseed add an unexpected note of licorice to a sophisticated combination of vegetables and prosciutto.

Broccoli, Sausage & Shells in Balsamic Sauce

Lovers of spicy food will relish the fiery
jolt provided by hot Italian sausage
and crushed red pepper.

Preparation Time: 20 minutes
Cooking Time: 22 to 23 minutes

INGREDIENTS

6	OUNCES CONCHIGLIE, CAVATELLI, *OR* OTHER DRIED SHELL-SHAPED PASTA
4	CUPS BROCCOLI FLOWERETS
12	OUNCES HOT ITALIAN SAUSAGE LINKS
1	TABLESPOON OLIVE OIL *OR* COOKING OIL
2	CLOVES GARLIC, PEELED
1	TABLESPOON ALL-PURPOSE FLOUR
1/8	TO 1/4 TEASPOON CRUSHED RED PEPPER
1	CUP CHICKEN BROTH
2	TABLESPOONS BALSAMIC VINEGAR

69

*I*talian balsamic vinegar is aged for years
in wooden barrels to mellow and sweeten.
*Look for this unique condiment in specialty foods
stores and well-stocked supermarkets.*

■ In a large saucepan or pasta pot bring 3 quarts water to
boiling. Add pasta. Reduce heat slightly. Boil, uncovered, for
12 to 14 minutes, or till pasta is al dente, stirring occasionally.
Add broccoli to the pan during the last 5 minutes of cooking. (Or,
cook according to package directions, adding broccoli the last 5 minutes.) Immediately drain. Return pasta and broccoli to warm pan.

STEPS AT A GLANCE	Page
CUTTING FLOWERETS	36
COOKING PASTA	12

■ Meanwhile, in a large skillet cook sausage links, covered, in ½ cup boiling water for 15
minutes. Drain off liquid in skillet. Add olive oil and garlic to sausages in skillet and cook,
uncovered, for 4 to 5 minutes, turning sausages to brown them on all sides. Remove from
heat. Discard garlic and reserve 1 tablespoon of the pan drippings in the skillet. Cool sausage
links, then bias-slice into ¼-inch-thick pieces.

■ Stir flour and crushed red pepper into reserved drippings in skillet. Add chicken broth all
at once. Cook and stir over medium heat till thickened and bubbly. Cook and stir for 2 minutes more. Stir in balsamic vinegar. Pour chicken broth mixture over pasta-broccoli mixture.
Add sausage and toss to mix well; heat through. Serve immediately.

Makes 4 main-dish servings

Per serving: 460 calories, 23 g protein, 45 g carbohydrate, 21 g total fat (6 g saturated), 49 mg cholesterol, 804 mg sodium,
629 mg potassium

Rigatoni with Sausage & Mushroom Sauce

INGREDIENTS

1	POUND BULK ITALIAN SAUSAGE
1	CUP SLICED FRESH MUSHROOMS
1/2	CUP CHOPPED ONION
1	15-OUNCE CAN TOMATO SAUCE
1/2	CUP DRY WHITE OR RED WINE
2	TABLESPOONS SNIPPED FRESH PARSLEY
1	TEASPOON DRIED ITALIAN SEASONING, CRUSHED
1/2	TEASPOON SALT
1/4	TEASPOON PEPPER
8	OUNCES RIGATONI, PENNE, OR OTHER DRIED SHAPED PASTA

Preparation Time: 15 minutes
Cooking Time: 45 to 50 minutes

STEPS AT A GLANCE	Page
PREPARING SAUCE INGREDIENTS	16
BROWNING MEAT	21
SIMMERING SAUCE	18
COOKING PASTA	12

*R*ib-sticking and chunky, this is an ideal cold-weather meal, perfect for hungry skiers, sledders, and skaters. Offer a glass of red wine alongside.*

■ In a large skillet cook sausage, mushrooms, and onion for 5 minutes, or till sausage is brown and onion and mushrooms are tender. Drain off fat. Add the tomato sauce, wine, parsley, Italian seasoning, salt, and pepper. Bring to boiling; reduce heat. Cover and simmer for 30 minutes. Uncover and simmer for 10 to 15 minutes more, or to desired consistency, stirring occasionally.

■ Meanwhile, in a large saucepan or pasta pot bring 3 quarts water to boiling. Add pasta. Reduce heat slightly. Boil, uncovered, for 14 to 15 minutes, or till al dente, stirring occasionally. (Or, cook according to package directions.) Immediately drain, then pour sauce over hot cooked pasta and serve.

Makes 4 main-dish servings

Per serving: 566 calories, 27 g protein, 57 g carbohydrate, 23 g total fat (8 g saturated), 66 mg cholesterol, 1,713 mg sodium, 822 mg potassium

70

Not fancy, but eminently satisfying: sausage, mushrooms, wine, and onions bound together in a hearty tomato sauce.

Baked Pasta & Cheddar with Ham

With the addition of chopped ham and vegetables, baked macaroni and cheese expands to a full-course meal that will satisfy everyone, young and old.

Preparation Time: 30 minutes
Baking Time: 30 minutes

INGREDIENTS

8	OUNCES TRICOLORED *OR* PLAIN ROTINI *OR* OTHER DRIED SHAPED PASTA
1	MEDIUM CARROT, CUT INTO THIN, BITE-SIZE STRIPS
1/4	CUP CHOPPED ONION
1/4	CUP MARGARINE *OR* BUTTER
1/3	CUP ALL-PURPOSE FLOUR
1/4	TEASPOON PEPPER
3	CUPS MILK
3/4	CUP SHREDDED CHEDDAR CHEESE (3 OUNCES)
1/2	CUP SHREDDED AMERICAN CHEESE (2 OUNCES)
1/2	CUP CHOPPED GREEN SWEET PEPPER
1/2	CUP CHOPPED RED SWEET PEPPER
2	CUPS CHOPPED FULLY COOKED HAM
1/4	CUP SHREDDED CHEDDAR CHEESE (1 OUNCE)
	PEPPER (OPTIONAL)

71

*C*hopped carrots and sweet peppers add a festive sprinkling of color to this cheerful and easy casserole. It's a meal in itself with a side dish of steamed vegetables.

■ In a large saucepan or pasta pot bring 3 quarts water to boiling. Add pasta. Reduce heat slightly. Boil, uncovered, for 8 to 10 minutes, or till pasta is al dente, stirring occasionally. Add carrot to boiling pasta the last 2 minutes of cooking. (Or, cook according to package directions, adding carrot the last 2 minutes.) Immediately drain.

■ Meanwhile, in a large saucepan cook onion in margarine or butter for 5 minutes, or till tender but not brown. Stir in flour and pepper. Add milk all at once. Cook and stir till slightly thickened and bubbly. Add ¾ cup cheddar cheese and ½ cup American cheese; stir till melted. Stir in pasta-carrot mixture, green and red sweet pepper, and ham.

■ Transfer mixture to a 2-quart round casserole. Bake, covered, in a preheated 350° oven for 25 minutes. Remove from oven and sprinkle with ¼ cup cheddar cheese and pepper, if desired. Return to oven and bake, uncovered, for 5 minutes more.

Makes 6 main-dish servings

Per serving: 476 calories, 26 g protein, 44 g carbohydrate, 21 g total fat (9 g saturated), 48 mg cholesterol, 933 mg sodium, 495 mg potassium

STEPS AT A GLANCE	Page
COOKING PASTA	12

Neapolitan Sauce with Penne

Unmistakably Italian, this sauce features
capers, anchovies, ripe olives, and other
Mediterranean flavors.

Preparation Time: 15 minutes
Cooking Time: 20 minutes

INGREDIENTS

1/3	CUP FINELY CHOPPED ONION
2	CLOVES GARLIC, MINCED
1	TABLESPOON OLIVE OIL OR COOKING OIL
1	28-OUNCE CAN WHOLE ITALIAN-STYLE TOMATOES, CUT UP
2	TABLESPOONS SNIPPED FRESH OREGANO OR 2 TEASPOONS DRIED OREGANO, CRUSHED
2	TABLESPOONS TOMATO PASTE
1	TABLESPOON CAPERS, DRAINED AND RINSED
1	TEASPOON SUGAR
1	TEASPOON ANCHOVY PASTE
1/8	TO 1/4 TEASPOON GROUND RED PEPPER
6	OUNCES PENNE, RIGATONI, OR OTHER DRIED SHAPED PASTA
1/4	CUP KALAMATA OLIVES, PITTED AND CHOPPED, OR PITTED RIPE OLIVES, CHOPPED
2	TABLESPOONS SNIPPED FRESH PARSLEY

72

A tiny bit of anchovy paste helps give the sauce
for this pasta dish the inimitable flavor of
Southern Italian cooking.

■ In a large saucepan cook the onion and garlic in hot oil till onion is tender but not
brown. Stir in the undrained tomatoes, oregano, tomato paste, capers, sugar, anchovy
paste, and red pepper. Bring to boiling; reduce heat. Simmer, uncovered, for about 20
minutes, or to desired consistency.

■ Meanwhile, in a large saucepan or pasta pot bring 3 quarts water to boiling. Add pasta.
Reduce heat slightly. Boil, uncovered, 14 to 15 minutes, or till al dente, stirring occasionally.
(Or, cook according to package directions.) Immediately drain. Return pasta to warm pan.

■ Pour tomato mixture and olives over hot cooked pasta and toss to coat pasta. Transfer
to a warm serving dish. Sprinkle with parsley and serve immediately.
Makes 6 side-dish servings

Per serving: 179 calories, 6 g protein, 31 g carbohydrate, 4 g total fat (1 g saturated), 1 mg cholesterol, 304 mg sodium,
414 mg potassium

Broccoli & Pasta in Garlic Butter

Preparation Time: 15 minutes
Cooking Time: 12 to 14 minutes

INGREDIENTS

4	OUNCES RUOTE, CONCHIGLIE *OR* OTHER DRIED SHAPED PASTA
2	CUPS BROCCOLI *OR* CAULIFLOWER FLOWERETS
1	TABLESPOON SNIPPED FRESH BASIL, *OR* 1/2 TEASPOON DRIED BASIL, CRUSHED
2	CLOVES GARLIC, HALVED LENGTHWISE
2	TABLESPOONS MARGARINE *OR* BUTTER
2	TABLESPOONS OLIVE OIL *OR* COOKING OIL
1/4	CUP GRATED ROMANO *OR* PARMESAN CHEESE
	PEPPER (OPTIONAL)

*C*ombine crisp flowerets of broccoli or cauliflower with little pasta wheels for an easy but delicious side dish that contrasts crisp and al dente textures. Another time, try the hybrid vegetable Broccoflower instead.

■ In a large saucepan or pasta pot bring 3 quarts water to boiling. Add pasta. Reduce heat slightly. Boil, uncovered, for 12 to 14 minutes, or till al dente, stirring occasionally. (Or, cook according to package directions.) Immediately drain.

■ Meanwhile, in a medium saucepan cook broccoli or cauliflower flowerets and basil, covered, in a small amount of boiling salted water for 6 to 8 minutes or till crisp-tender. Drain well. In a large skillet cook the garlic in hot margarine or butter and olive oil or cooking oil for about 5 minutes, or till garlic is golden, stirring occasionally. Remove garlic from skillet and discard.

■ Add broccoli or cauliflower flowerets to warm skillet and toss to coat with margarine-oil mixture; heat through. Add hot cooked pasta and Romano or Parmesan cheese and toss to mix. Transfer to a warm serving dish. If desired, sprinkle with pepper. Serve immediately.

Makes 4 side-dish servings

Per serving: 271 calories, 8 g protein, 27 g carbohydrate, 15 g total fat (3 g saturated), 7 mg cholesterol, 173 mg sodium, 269 mg potassium

73

A simple sauce of butter, olive oil, garlic, and broccoli is tossed with ruote (wagon-wheel pasta).

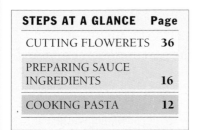

White Cheese & Macaroni

INGREDIENTS

1	CUP ELBOW MACARONI OR DITALINI (4 OUNCES)
1	LARGE CLOVE GARLIC, CUT LENGTHWISE INTO SLIVERS
1/3	CUP MILK
1	TABLESPOON MARGARINE OR BUTTER
1	CUP SHREDDED SHARP WHITE CHEDDAR CHEESE
1/4	TEASPOON WHITE OR BLACK PEPPER
1	TABLESPOON SNIPPED FRESH PARSLEY

Preparation Time: 15 minutes
Cooking Time: 10 to 13 minutes

STEPS AT A GLANCE	Page
COOKING PASTA	12

*T*he pasta can be cooked ahead, if you prefer. Drain, toss in a little oil, cover, and set aside for up to 2 hours or until needed. When preparing the sauce, return the cooked pasta to the saucepan, add the remaining ingredients, and finish the recipe as directed.

■ In a large saucepan or pasta pot bring 3 quarts water to boiling. Add pasta and garlic slivers. Reduce heat slightly. Boil, uncovered, for 8 to 10 minutes, or till al dente, stirring occasionally. (Or, cook according to package directions.) Immediately drain.

■ Return pasta and garlic to warm pan. Add milk. Cook on low heat for 2 to 3 minutes, or till all of the milk is absorbed by the pasta. Add margarine or butter, cheese, and pepper. Stir mixture gently till cheese is melted. Garnish with parsley and serve immediately.

Makes 4 side-dish servings

Per serving: 275 calories, 12 g protein, 27 g carbohydrate, 13 g total fat (7 g saturated), 31 mg cholesterol, 221 mg sodium, 97 mg potassium

Sharp white cheddar cheese and slivers of garlic transform a childhood favorite into a grown-up accompaniment for grilled fish or meat.

Layered Pasta

Steps for Making Layered Pasta

BAKING DISH

Basic Tools for Layering Pasta

Equipment for preparing and serving layered pasta casseroles includes a chef's knife, assorted bowls, and spatulas. A pastry wheel and ruler are helpful when cutting fresh lasagne noodles.

CUTTING BOARD
AND GLASS BOWLS

CHEF'S KNIFE

FLUTED PASTRY WHEEL

RULER

METAL SPATULA

LARGE, WIDE SPATULA

76

L ASAGNE MADE WITH packaged noodles, cheese, and tomato-meat sauce is probably the most familiar layered pasta, but by no means the only one, as you will discover in this chapter. The steps and recipes that follow clearly demonstrate that layered pasta is a whole category of tempting recipes, not just a single dish.

The ingredients make the difference; the technique varies only slightly. Each is a construction of pasta and filling, with every layer contrasting yet complementing the others. Each is assembled in an ovenproof dish and baked until piping hot from top to bottom. All are hearty, satisfying, and good for casual company meals because they can be prepared in advance and reheated.

Lasagne Verdi, page 86, is a classic dish made with fresh or dried spinach noodles. Salmon Lasagne with Roasted Pepper Sauce, page 81, is a contemporary seafood casserole, and Vegetable Lasagne, page 84, dispenses with meat altogether to showcase a cornucopia of vegetables. Three recipes use shaped pasta rather than flat sheets: Four Seasons Pasta Pie, page 78, has a spaghetti "crust," while both Greek-inspired Pastitsio, page 82, and Spicy Sausage & Corn Pasta, page 85, include macaroni.

dried pasta may be substituted for fresh pasta in layered dishes

STEP 1 CUTTING FRESH LASAGNE NOODLES
Let the rolled fresh dough rest for about 20 minutes to dry slightly. Trim each piece to a large rectangle, as specified in the recipe. With a fluted pastry wheel or a sharp knife, cut each rectangle into even strips, using a ruler as a guide.

fresh noodles need only to
be cooked briefly before
layering

you can also use a rubber spatula or wooden spoon to spread
the cheese or filling

vary the recipe by using other
kinds of shredded cheeses

STEP 2 SETTING THE NOODLES ASIDE

If necessary, trim the strips further to the size specified in the recipe. Place the strips on slightly damp kitchen towels so they won't overdry while you are cutting the remaining rectangles of dough. After cooking the noodles, place them on the towels to keep them from sticking together.

STEP 3 ASSEMBLING THE DISH

Cover the bottom of the dish with a little sauce to keep the noodles from sticking to the pan. Top with noodles, more sauce, and grated cheeses. Add the next layer of noodles. With a metal spat-ula, spread ricotta cheese or filling evenly across the noodles.

STEP 4 SPRINKLING WITH CHEESE

Arrange a layer of noodles over the filling. Spoon on the remaining sauce and spread to cover the pasta. Finish layering by sprinkling with the remaining cheeses.

77

the casserole will cut more easily
if allowed to rest first to let the
layers cool and set

Layers of fresh spinach pasta alter-nate with creamy cheeses and a rich meat sauce to make hearty Lasagne Verdi (page 86).

STEP 5 CUTTING INTO SERVINGS

Remove lasagne from the oven and let sit for 10 minutes. Cut into serving-size portions with a sharp knife. Transfer each portion to individual plates with a large, wide spatula.

Four Seasons Pasta Pie

Preparation Time: 30 minutes
Baking Time: 25 minutes

INGREDIENTS

CRUST

5	OUNCES DRIED SPAGHETTI OR LINGUINE OR 10 OUNCES FRESH LINGUINE
1	BEATEN EGG
1/4	CUP GRATED PARMESAN CHEESE
1	TABLESPOON MARGARINE OR BUTTER

CHEESE FILLING

1	BEATEN EGG
1	CUP RICOTTA CHEESE
1/8	TEASPOON PEPPER

TOPPING

1/2	CUP SLICED FRESH MUSHROOMS
1	TEASPOON OLIVE OIL
1	OUNCE PROSCIUTTO OR FULLY COOKED HAM, CHOPPED (1/4 CUP)
2	PLUM TOMATOES, THINLY SLICED
4	TEASPOONS PESTO (PAGE 22)
2	TABLESPOONS GRATED PARMESAN CHEESE

78

If fresh plum tomatoes aren't in season, peel and thinly slice 1 large tomato, then cut the slices in half and arrange on top of the prosciutto or ham.

■ For crust, in a large saucepan or pasta pot bring 3 quarts water to boiling. Add pasta. Reduce heat slightly. Boil, uncovered, 8 to 12 minutes for dried pasta or 1½ to 2 minutes for fresh, or till al dente, stirring occasionally. (Or, cook according to package directions.) Immediately drain. Return to warm pan.

■ Meanwhile, in a medium mixing bowl combine egg, Parmesan cheese, and margarine or butter. Pour over hot spaghetti in saucepan and toss to coat. Press spaghetti mixture evenly into bottom and up sides of a well-greased 9-inch pie plate. Set aside.

■ For cheese filling, in a small mixing bowl combine egg, ricotta cheese, and pepper. Spread over spaghetti crust.

■ For topping, in a medium skillet cook and stir mushrooms in hot oil for 2 minutes, or till tender. Set aside. Sprinkle chopped prosciutto or ham over cheese filling. Arrange tomato slices in a circle 1 inch from the edge of the pie plate. Dot pesto on tomato slices. Arrange mushrooms inside the circle of tomatoes.

■ Cover and bake in a preheated 350° oven for 20 minutes. Uncover and sprinkle with Parmesan cheese. Bake, uncovered, for about 5 minutes more, or till cheese melts. Let stand for 5 to 10 minutes before serving. Cut into wedges to serve.

Makes 4 main-dish servings

Per serving: 513 calories, 27 g protein, 53 g carbohydrate, 21 g total fat (7 g saturated), 195 mg cholesterol, 495 mg sodium, 282 mg potassium

STEPS AT A GLANCE	Page
COOKING PASTA	12
MAKING PESTO	22
MAKING PASTA PIE	78

STEPS FOR MAKING PASTA PIE

STEP 1 FORMING THE CRUST
With the back of a wooden spoon, press the spaghetti-egg mixture evenly against the bottom and sides of a well-greased 9-inch pie plate.

STEP 2 DOTTING WITH PESTO
Spread the ricotta cheese mixture over the crust and top with the prosciutto or ham and tomatoes. Scoop up the pesto with a small spoon and push it off with a small spatula onto the tomatoes. Top with a ring of sautéed sliced mushrooms.

This savory dinner pie has a spaghetti "crust," a peppery cheese filling, and a topping of pesto, prosciutto or ham, mushrooms, and tomatoes.

Roasted sweet peppers delicately tint and flavor the top layer of a seafood-and-pesto lasagne.

Salmon Lasagne with Roasted Pepper Sauce

Preparation Time: 1½ hours
Baking Time: 30 to 35 minutes

INGREDIENTS

12	OUNCES SKINLESS FRESH OR FROZEN SALMON FILLETS OR TWO 6-1/8-OUNCE CANS BONELESS, SKINLESS SALMON, DRAINED AND BROKEN UP
2	LARGE RED SWEET PEPPERS
1/3	CUP PESTO (PAGE 22)
9	DRIED LASAGNE NOODLES
1/2	CUP DAIRY SOUR CREAM
1	TABLESPOON ALL-PURPOSE FLOUR
1/4	TEASPOON SALT
1/8	TEASPOON PEPPER
1	BEATEN EGG
1	CUP RICOTTA CHEESE
1	8-OUNCE PACKAGE CREAM CHEESE, SOFTENED

*R*oasted red peppers have a completely different flavor from fresh ones. To use fresh lasagne noodles for this dish, follow the directions in the recipe on page 86, using 3 portions homemade pasta to make 9 noodles.

■ Thaw salmon, if frozen. Halve the red sweet peppers; remove stems, seeds, and membranes. Place peppers, cut-sides down, on a foil-lined baking sheet. Bake in a preheated 425° oven for 20 to 25 minutes, or till skins are blistered and dark. Remove from baking sheet. Immediately place in a paper bag. Close bag; let stand about 30 minutes to steam the peppers so skins peel away more easily. (Or, place the bag in the freezer for 5 to 10 minutes.) Using a sharp knife, remove the skin from the peppers, pulling it off in strips. Discard skins. Reduce oven temperature to 375°.

■ Meanwhile, prepare pesto as directed. Set aside. If using fresh or thawed frozen salmon fillets, in a large skillet bring about 1½ cups water to boiling. Meanwhile, measure the thickness of the salmon fillets. Add salmon to skillet. Return just to boiling and reduce heat. Cover and simmer for 4 to 6 minutes per ½-inch thickness. Drain, discarding cooking liquid. Use a fork to break fish into bite-size pieces. Set aside.

■ In a large saucepan or pasta pot bring 3 quarts water to boiling. Add pasta. Reduce heat slightly. Boil, uncovered, for 10 to 12 minutes, or till al dente, stirring occasionally. (Or, cook according to package directions.) Immediately drain. Rinse with cold water; drain again.

■ In a food processor bowl or blender container, process or blend the roasted peppers till nearly smooth. Add sour cream, flour, salt, and pepper. Process or blend till combined. Set aside.

■ In a medium mixing bowl combine egg, ricotta cheese, and cream cheese. Stir in pesto and cooked or canned salmon.

■ To assemble, lightly grease a 2-quart rectangular baking dish. Arrange 3 of the noodles in the bottom of the dish. Spread with one third (about 1¼ cups) of the cheese mixture. Repeat layers twice. Carefully spread roasted red pepper mixture over the top layer.

■ Bake, uncovered, in a 375° oven for 30 to 35 minutes, or till heated through. Let stand for 10 minutes before serving.

Makes 8 main-dish servings

Per serving: 386 calories, 17 g protein, 24 g carbohydrate, 25 g total fat (10 g saturated), 83 mg cholesterol, 309 mg sodium, 209 mg potassium

---

STEPS FOR ROASTING PEPPERS AND POACHING SALMON

STEP 1 ROASTING PEPPERS

Place stemmed and seeded pepper halves on a foil-lined baking sheet. Roast in a preheated 425° oven until the skins are blistered.

STEP 2 PEELING PEPPERS

After cooling the peppers, peel away the skin by pulling it off in strips with a sharp paring knife.

STEP 3 POACHING SALMON

Cook salmon in barely simmering water for 4 to 6 minutes per ½-inch thickness of fish. When done, lift out carefully with a wide spatula.

Pastitsio

Preparation Time: 45 minutes (includes sauce)
Baking Time: 30 to 35 minutes

INGREDIENTS

MEAT SAUCE (PAGE 47)

PASTA

8	OUNCES ELBOW MACARONI (2 CUPS)
1	BEATEN EGG
1/4	CUP GRATED PARMESAN CHEESE

WHITE SAUCE

3	TABLESPOONS MARGARINE OR BUTTER
3	TABLESPOONS ALL-PURPOSE FLOUR
1/4	TEASPOON PEPPER
1-1/2	CUPS MILK
1	BEATEN EGG
1/4	CUP GRATED PARMESAN CHEESE
	GROUND CINNAMON (OPTIONAL)

The white sauce firms up into a creamy, delicious layer, and the cinnamon adds an exotic flavor to this traditional Greek dish.

- Prepare the meat sauce as directed. Set aside.

- For pasta, in a large saucepan or pasta pot bring 3 quarts water to boiling. Add pasta. Reduce heat slightly. Boil, uncovered, for about 10 minutes, or till al dente, stirring occasionally. (Or, cook according to package directions.) Immediately drain. Rinse with cold water. Drain again.

- In a large mixing bowl combine 1 beaten egg, ¼ cup Parmesan cheese, and hot cooked macaroni. Set aside.

- For white sauce, in a medium saucepan melt margarine or butter. Stir in flour and pepper. Add the milk all at once. Cook and stir till thickened and bubbly. Stir about half of the mixture into 1 beaten egg. Return egg mixture to the saucepan. Stir in ¼ cup Parmesan cheese.

- To assemble, layer half of the pasta mixture in a greased 2-quart square baking dish. Top with all of the meat sauce, the remaining pasta mixture, and all of the white sauce. If desired, sprinkle lightly with cinnamon.

- Bake in a preheated 350° oven for 30 to 35 minutes, or till set. Let stand for 5 minutes before serving.

Makes 6 main-dish servings

Per serving: 429 calories, 26 g protein, 45 g carbohydrate, 16 g total fat (5 g saturated), 118 mg cholesterol, 672 mg sodium, 660 mg potassium

82

STEPS FOR LAYERING PASTITSIO

STEP 1 MAKING PASTA MIXTURE

Cook the macaroni, then drain thoroughly. In a large mixing bowl, combine the pasta with the egg and grated Parmesan cheese. Mix well.

STEP 2 LAYERING

Spread half of the pasta mixture on the bottom of a 2-quart baking dish. Cover with the meat sauce. Then, spoon on the remaining pasta so that it covers the sauce completely. Top with all the white sauce.

A simple vegetable accompaniment such as grilled eggplant and fresh tomato wedges will nicely complement this traditional Greek pasta casserole.

Vegetable Lasagne

*T*o *prepare this dish with fresh lasagne noodles, follow the directions in the recipe on page 86, using 2 portions of homemade pasta. If you want to use fresh artichoke hearts, prepare them as directed on page 59, then blanch them for about 5 minutes.*

■ In a large saucepan or pasta pot bring 3 quarts water to boiling. Add pasta. Reduce heat slightly. Boil, uncovered, for 10 to 12 minutes, or till al dente, stirring occasionally. (Or, cook according to package directions.) Immediately drain. Rinse with cold water; drain again.

■ For vegetables, cook artichoke hearts according to package directions. Drain and chop. In a large skillet cook mushrooms and carrots in margarine or butter for 3 minutes, or till tender. Stir in chopped artichoke hearts. Set vegetable mixture aside.

■ For sauce, in a medium saucepan cook green onion and garlic in hot margarine or butter till tender. Stir in flour and pepper. Add half-and-half, light cream, or milk and chicken broth all at once. Cook and stir till thickened and bubbly. Remove from heat and set aside. For filling, in a medium mixing bowl combine spinach, cottage cheese, and Parmesan cheese; set aside.

■ To assemble, grease a 2-quart rectangular baking dish. Arrange 3 noodles in the prepared dish. Spread half of the filling on top of the noodles. Spoon half of the vegetable mixture over the filling. Spoon half of the sauce over top. Repeat layers.

■ Bake, covered, in a preheated 350° oven for 35 minutes. Uncover and sprinkle ¼ cup Parmesan cheese over the top. Bake for 5 to 10 minutes more, or till mixture is heated through. Let stand for 10 minutes before serving.

Makes 8 main-dish servings

84

Per serving: 233 calories, 13 g protein, 26 g carbohydrate, 10 g total fat (4 g saturated), 18 mg cholesterol, 415 mg sodium, 471 mg potassium

STEPS AT A GLANCE	Page
COOKING PASTA	12
PREPARING SAUCE INGREDIENTS	16
MAKING LAYERED PASTA	76

Preparation Time: 40 minutes
Baking Time: 40 to 45 minutes

INGREDIENTS

6	DRIED LASAGNE NOODLES

VEGETABLES

1	9-OUNCE PACKAGE FROZEN ARTICHOKE HEARTS
3	CUPS SLICED FRESH MUSHROOMS (8 OUNCES)
1	CUP SHREDDED CARROTS
1	TABLESPOON MARGARINE *OR* BUTTER

SAUCE

1/2	CUP SLICED GREEN ONIONS
2	CLOVES GARLIC, MINCED
1	TABLESPOON MARGARINE *OR* BUTTER
1/4	CUP ALL-PURPOSE FLOUR
1/4	TEASPOON PEPPER
1	CUP HALF-AND-HALF, LIGHT CREAM, *OR* MILK
3/4	CUP CHICKEN BROTH

FILLING

1	10-OUNCE PACKAGE FROZEN CHOPPED SPINACH, THAWED AND WELL DRAINED
1	CUP CREAM-STYLE COTTAGE CHEESE, DRAINED
1/4	CUP GRATED PARMESAN CHEESE

TOPPING

1/4	CUP GRATED PARMESAN CHEESE

Chunky vegetables such as artichoke hearts, mushrooms, and carrots add appealing texture and crunch to a meatless lasagne.

Spicy Sausage & Corn Pasta

Preparation Time: 30 minutes
Baking Time: 30 to 45 minutes

INGREDIENTS

12	OUNCES REDUCED-FAT TURKEY AND PORK SAUSAGE *OR* TURKEY SAUSAGE
1/2	CUP CHOPPED ONION
1	CLOVE GARLIC, MINCED
1	15-OUNCE CAN TOMATO SAUCE
1	CUP WATER
2	TABLESPOONS SNIPPED FRESH CILANTRO (OPTIONAL)
1	TABLESPOON TOMATO PASTE
1/2	TEASPOON SALT
1/2	TEASPOON GROUND CUMIN
1/4	TEASPOON CHILI POWDER
1/4	TEASPOON GROUND CORIANDER
1/8	TEASPOON GROUND RED PEPPER
4	OUNCES CORN *OR* PLAIN ELBOW MACARONI (1 CUP)
1/2	OF A 15-OUNCE CAN PINTO BEANS, DRAINED, *OR* 1 CUP COOKED DRIED PINTO BEANS, DRAINED
1	CUP SHREDDED MONTEREY JACK CHEESE (4 OUNCES)

85

*I*f you like Mexican food, here's a one-dish meal chock-full of all your favorite Mexican ingredients. Choose Monterey jack cheese with jalapeño peppers for extra heat. Look for the corn elbow macaroni at a health food store; it is often used by people on wheat-free diets.

■ In a large skillet cook the sausage, onion, and garlic for 5 minutes, or till meat is brown. Drain off fat. Add tomato sauce, water, cilantro (if desired), tomato paste, salt, cumin, chili powder, coriander, and red pepper. Bring to boiling; reduce heat. Cover and simmer for 15 minutes.

■ Lightly grease a 2-quart square baking dish. Layer half of the uncooked elbow macaroni, half of the sausage mixture, half of the pinto beans, and half of the cheese. Repeat layers.

■ Bake, covered, in a preheated 350° oven for 20 minutes (40 minutes for plain macaroni). Uncover and bake for 10 minutes more (5 minutes more for plain macaroni), or till pasta is tender and mixture is heated through. Let stand for 10 minutes before serving.

Makes 6 main-dish servings

Per serving: 327 calories, 19 g protein, 26 g carbohydrate, 18 g total fat (4 g saturated), 17 mg cholesterol, 826 mg sodium, 403 mg potassium

A fruit garnish of juicy orange wedges and tart-sweet kiwifruit helps to cool the fire of a spicy Mexican pasta main course.

STEPS AT A GLANCE	Page
PREPARING SAUCE INGREDIENTS	16
SIMMERING SAUCE	18
LAYERING	82

Lasagne Verdi

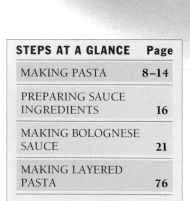

This appealing lasagne displays all the colors of the Italian flag: green spinach noodles, creamy white cheese, and tomato-red sauce.

Preparation Time: 1¼ hours (includes sauce)
Baking Time: 30 minutes

INGREDIENTS

9	DRIED SPINACH OR PLAIN LASAGNE NOODLES *OR* 3 PORTIONS HOMEMADE PASTA (PAGE 14)
	BOLOGNESE SAUCE (PAGE 21)
2	TABLESPOONS MARGARINE *OR* BUTTER
2	TABLESPOONS ALL-PURPOSE FLOUR
1/4	TEASPOON SALT
	DASH PEPPER
2/3	CUP MILK
1/2	CUP RICOTTA CHEESE
2	CUPS SHREDDED MOZZARELLA CHEESE (8 OUNCES)
1/4	CUP GRATED PARMESAN CHEESE

*I*n Italian, verdi *means "green," and green spinach pasta is what gives our recipe its name. You can use plain pasta if you prefer.*

■ If using homemade pasta, roll each portion of dough to a 12x9-inch rectangle. Cut into three 12x2½-inch noodles.

■ Prepare Bolognese sauce, except omit the whipping cream and nutmeg. Set aside. In a small saucepan melt margarine or butter. Stir in flour, salt, and pepper. Add milk all at once. Cook and stir over medium heat till thickened and bubbly. Stir in ricotta cheese.

■ In a large saucepan or pasta pot bring 3 quarts water to boiling. Add pasta. Reduce heat slightly. Boil, uncovered, for 10 to 12 minutes for dried pasta or 2 to 3 minutes for fresh, or till al dente, stirring occasionally. (Or, cook according to package directions.) Immediately drain. Rinse with cold water; drain again.

■ Spread ½ cup of the Bolognese sauce in the bottom of a greased 2-quart rectangular baking dish. Arrange one third of the noodles on top of the sauce. Spread with half of the remaining Bolognese sauce. Sprinkle with half of the mozzarella and half of the Parmesan. Add another layer of noodles and all of the ricotta mixture. Repeat layers with remaining noodles, Bolognese sauce, mozzarella, and Parmesan.

■ Bake, uncovered, in a preheated 375° oven for 30 minutes, or till heated through. Let stand for 10 minutes before serving.

Makes 6 to 8 main-dish servings

Per serving: 534 calories, 33 g protein, 47 g carbohydrate, 23 g total fat (10 g saturated), 70 mg cholesterol, 732 mg sodium, 878 mg potassium

86

Stuffed Pasta

Steps for Stuffing Pasta

SMALL AND
MEDIUM BOWLS

RAVIOLI FRAME

ROLLING PIN

SOFT PAINTBRUSH

MEASURING
TEASPOON

CUTTING BOARD

FLUTED
PASTRY WHEEL

BASIC TOOLS FOR MAKING STUFFED PASTA

A ravioli frame allows for assembly-line efficiency when filling, sealing, and scoring pasta squares, but it is almost as easy to shape them by hand and cut them with a pastry wheel. Bowls and a measuring spoon are also necessary for stuffing pasta, and a small paintbrush is helpful for sealing.

ALTHOUGH DELICATE AND TENDER, fresh pasta is sturdy enough to serve as edible wrapping for all sorts of tasty bundles. Some enclose the filling completely so that the first bite is a delicious surprise. These include square ravioli, half-moon-shaped agnolotti, and ring-shaped tortellini. Tubular cannelloni and manicotti — discussed on page 90 — and their close kin the pasta roll (see Stuffed Pasta Rolls, page 92) are left partially open to reveal some of the savory mixture encased within.

Classic fillings incorporate cheeses like creamy ricotta and pungent grated Parmesan, and chopped spinach or ham, all bound with a little egg. Others feature meaty mushrooms, spicy sausage seasoned with herbs, or intensely flavorful dried tomatoes. These pastas and fillings nicely mix and match, so you can experiment and interchange them for variety.

Regardless of their final form, all of these packages begin with a basic pasta dough rolled by hand or with a machine into thin sheets as for lasagne or ribbon pasta. To review this technique, see Steps for Making Pasta, pages 8 through 11. Unlike ribbon pasta, however, pasta for stuffing must be pliable. Don't let the rolled sheet dry or you won't be able to shape it. Use immediately and cover unused portions with a kitchen towel or plastic wrap until needed.

Shape and fill ravioli and tortellini assembly-line fashion. Always leave a sufficient margin of dough around the filling to ensure a good seal. For a different look, vary the size by using large, wide strips for ravioli or bigger circles for tortellini. A trio or quartet of 3-inch ravioli looks quite dramatic as a first course. Create an attractive edge on either ravioli or tortellini by cutting with a fluted pastry wheel or scalloped cutter.

Forming ravioli by hand is very easy, but a metal frame already molded with indentations and scoring notches will speed the process along. Most cookware stores or department-store houseware sections stock these. Both hand and frame methods for ravioli are shown in steps 1 through 4 at right.

Stuffed pasta can be made early in the day and cooked close to serving time. Arrange on a flour-dusted tray, lightly dust with flour, and refrigerate, covered with a kitchen towel. Don't let the pieces touch or they might stick together and tear when you try to separate them.

press out as much air as
possible around filling
before sealing

press down the edges
of the cut ravioli one
more time to seal

one teaspoonful is
about the proper
amount of filling

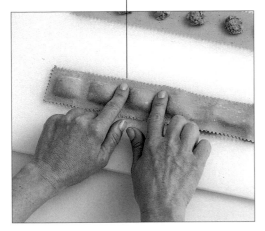

STEP 1 SEALING RAVIOLI

On each 2x12-inch strip of dough, arrange 1 tea-spoon of filling every 2 inches, beginning 1 inch from one end. Moisten the dough around the fill-ing with a small paintbrush or your finger, top with another strip of dough, and press down on either side of the filling to seal.

STEP 2 CUTTING RAVIOLI

With a fluted pastry cutter or sharp knife, cut halfway between the mounds of filling to sepa-rate the ravioli. Repeat with the remaining pasta and filling.

STEP 3 MAKING RAVIOLI WITH A FRAME

Drape a sheet of fresh dough on the bottom of the frame. Press lightly into each hollow, or set the top of the frame (if there is one) on the dough and press gently. Place about 1 teaspoon of filling in each hollow.

89

after sealing, remove the
ravioli from the frame and
pull them apart at the seams

you can work faster
if you fill a number of
circles at one time

if the dough has dried out,
moisten the ends before
you pinch them together

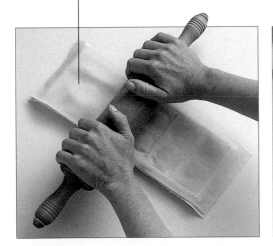

STEP 4 SEALING RAVIOLI IN A FRAME

Brush the dough lightly with water. Set another rectangle of dough on top of the filling. Using firm, even pressure, push a wooden rolling pin across. Or, apply the top of the frame, if there is one. This action both seals the ravioli and scores them.

STEP 5 FOLDING TORTELLINI

Stamp out little rounds of dough with a 1½-inch round cutter. Place about ¼ teaspoon filling in the center of each round. Brush the edge with water. Create a half-moon by folding the dough circle in half. Pinch along the edge to seal.

STEP 6 SHAPING TORTELLINI

Bend the half-moon, seam-side out, and bring the two outer ends together. Pinch them to seal. For larger tortellini, shape by placing a finger against the fold and bending around it; overlap the ends and pinch.

Steps for Stuffing Manicotti and Cannelloni

BASIC TOOLS FOR MANICOTTI AND CANNELLONI

A ruler and rolling cutter make quick work of dividing pasta sheets into uniform squares or rectangles. Use a small spoon to fill cooked tubes so that their delicate walls won't tear. An oven-proof baking dish holds the finished product.

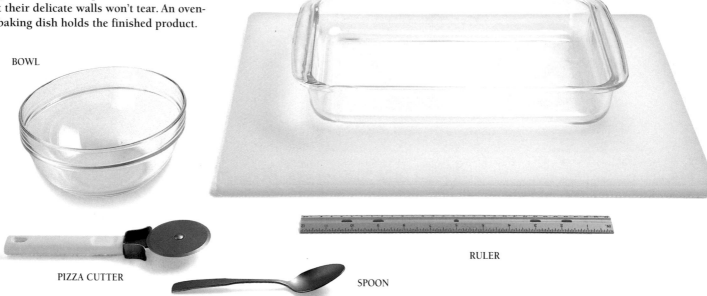

CUTTING BOARD AND BAKING DISH

BOWL

PIZZA CUTTER

RULER

SPOON

90

Manicotti and cannelloni are luscious rolls of pasta wrapped around cheese, meat, and vegetables. Both are easily assembled using paper-thin squares or rectangles of fresh dough or dried pasta tubes. The two are essentially the same dish with one difference: Manicotti is rolled on the diagonal, while cannelloni is rolled straight across. As seems to be true with all Italian pasta, even such a slight variation is inspiration for an entirely new name.

Both fresh pasta squares or rectangles and dried pasta tubes must be cooked in boiling water until just al dente. Don't overcook or overstuff dried pasta tubes, or they will burst as they expand during baking. For a more attractive shape, always roll cooked fresh pasta in a tight bundle around the filling.

Chicken-filled Classic Cannelloni, page 104, is topped with side-by-side tomato and cheese sauces. Broiled Spinach Cannelloni, page 103, is quickly browned under the broiler and covered with a lemony cream sauce. Manicotti with Roasted Vegetables, page 102, is baked with fresh tomato sauce and a topping of garlic-infused vegetables.

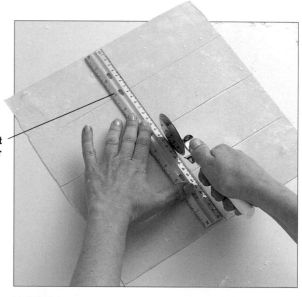

to make straight cuts, use a ruler as a guide

STEP 1 CUTTING PASTA SHEETS

Roll pasta into a thin sheet. Cut the sheet of dough into squares or rectangles, as directed in the recipe. Use a pizza cutter, a fluted pastry wheel, or a sharp knife.

use gentle pressure when rolling so the filling isn't squeezed out

fill from the center to the open end, then turn and fill the other end

some of the filling will be exposed at either end

STEP 2 FILLING CANNELLONI

Cook the pasta squares or rectangles until al dente. Drain and place on a kitchen towel. Spoon the filling along one edge of each cooked pasta piece. Roll the dough tightly around the filling.

STEP 3 FILLING DRIED MANICOTTI

Cook the shells until al dente. Drain and place on a kitchen towel. With a small spoon, carefully insert about ⅓ cup of filling into each shell; do not pack filling.

STEP 4 FILLING FRESH MANICOTTI

Cook the pasta rectangles until al dente. Drain and place on a kitchen towel. Place the rectangle with one corner toward you. Spoon about ⅓ cup filling diagonally across and just below the center of the rectangle. Beginning at the bottom corner, roll the dough around the filling.

91

set them seam-side down so they won't unroll

STEP 5 PLACING IN BAKING DISH

Carefully transfer filled cannelloni or manicotti to a baking dish. Arrange rolled pasta in the dish with the seams on the bottom.

Roll cooked pasta squares or rectangles around the filling of your choice, top with a simple tomato sauce and bake.

Stuffed Pasta Rolls

Preparation Time: 1½ hours
Baking Time: 20 minutes

INGREDIENTS

1	PORTION (4 OUNCES) SPINACH PASTA (PAGE 14)

FILLING

1/4	CUP FRESH CHIVES
1/4	CUP FRESH PARSLEY
1	OR 2 SMALL CLOVES GARLIC
1	8-OUNCE PACKAGE CREAM CHEESE
1/2	CUP CREAM-STYLE COTTAGE CHEESE
5	OUNCES THINLY SLICED CAPICOLLA, PROSCIUTTO, OR HAM
1/2	CUP DRAINED AND FINELY SNIPPED OIL-PACKED DRIED TOMATOES

SAUCE

2	CUPS SLICED FRESH MUSHROOMS
2	CLOVES GARLIC, MINCED
3	TABLESPOONS MARGARINE OR BUTTER
3	TABLESPOONS ALL-PURPOSE FLOUR
1/4	TEASPOON SALT
1/4	TEASPOON WHITE PEPPER
1	CUP CHICKEN BROTH
1	CUP HALF-AND-HALF, LIGHT CREAM, OR MILK
1/2	TEASPOON FINELY SHREDDED LEMON PEEL
1	TABLESPOON LEMON JUICE

*P*asta rolls are impressive to serve and surprisingly simple to make. When sliced, these reveal spirals of green pasta and a filling of ham, cheese, and chewy dried tomatoes. The rolls may be prepared 1 day ahead and refrigerated until ready to bake.

■ Prepare spinach pasta as directed, except divide the portion of dough in half and roll each half to a 12x6-inch rectangle. In a large saucepan or pasta pot bring 3 quarts water to boiling. Add 1 sheet of the pasta. Reduce heat slightly. Boil, uncovered, about 3 minutes, or till pasta is al dente, stirring occasionally. Use a slotted spoon to carefully lift pasta from water and into a colander. Rinse with cold water. Drain well. Carefully spread on a damp cloth towel. Repeat with remaining pasta sheet.

■ Meanwhile, for filling, in a food processor bowl or blender container finely chop the chives, parsley, and garlic. Add cream cheese and cottage cheese and blend till nearly smooth.

■ To assemble, spread half of the filling over each pasta sheet to within ¼ inch of the edges. Arrange the capicolla, prosciutto, or ham and snipped dried tomatoes in layers on top of the filling. Roll jelly-roll style, starting from one of the short sides. (If desired, cover pasta roll tightly and chill for up to 24 hours.) Trim uneven edges of rolls. Cut each roll into 6 slices. Place the slices, cut-side down, in a 2-quart rectangular baking dish. Bake, covered, in a pre-heated 375° oven for about 20 minutes, or till heated through.

■ Meanwhile, for sauce, in a medium saucepan cook mushrooms and garlic in hot margarine or butter till tender. Stir in flour, salt, and pepper. Add chicken broth and half-and-half, light cream, or milk all at once. Cook and stir till thickened and bubbly. Cook and stir for 1 minute more. Remove from heat and stir in lemon peel and lemon juice. To serve, divide sauce among individual plates. Arrange hot pasta pinwheels on top of sauce. Serve immediately.

Makes 4 to 6 main-dish servings

Per serving: 520 calories, 25 g protein, 30 g carbohydrate, 34 g total fat (16 g saturated), 104 mg cholesterol, 1,303 mg sodium, 787 mg potassium

STEPS FOR MAKING PASTA ROLLS

STEP 1 ROLLING PASTA
Begin at one short end. Roll pasta and filling jelly-roll style by rolling up the towel to gently push the dough along.

STEP 2 CUTTING PASTA
Trim away uneven ends of pasta rolls. Cut each roll into 6 slices with a serrated knife. Place the slices, cut-side down, in a baking dish. Cover with aluminum foil and bake as directed.

Colorful pinwheels of spinach
pasta and filling make a
stunning presentation.

94

Crisp lumpia are filled with a mixture of shrimp and pork flavored with spicy fresh ginger. Serve as an hors d'oeuvre or side dish with a garlicky dipping sauce.

Lumpia

INGREDIENTS

FILLING

1/2	CUP CHOPPED ONION
2	CLOVES GARLIC, MINCED
1	TEASPOON GRATED GINGERROOT
1	TABLESPOON COOKING OIL
3/4	CUP FINELY CHOPPED PEELED AND DEVEINED SHRIMP (ABOUT 12 MEDIUM)
3/4	CUP FINELY CHOPPED COOKED PORK (4 OUNCES)
1/4	CUP WATER
2	TABLESPOONS SOY SAUCE
1/8	TEASPOON PEPPER

SAUCE

2	CLOVES GARLIC, MINCED
1	TEASPOON COOKING OIL
1	TEASPOON CORNSTARCH
1/2	CUP VINEGAR
2	TABLESPOONS WATER

LUMPIA

12	LUMPIA WRAPPERS (FILIPINO PASTRY WRAPPERS) OR SPRING ROLL WRAPPERS
	COOKING OIL FOR FRYING

*F*ilipino-style egg rolls, or lumpia, are about 6 inches long and about as big around as a small cigar. Serve them as a delicious appetizer or side dish.

■ For filling, in a large skillet cook onion, garlic, and gingerroot in hot oil for 5 minutes, or till tender, but not brown. Add shrimp and cook till they turn pink, stirring constantly. Add cooked pork, water, soy sauce, and pepper. Cook till liquid is evaporated.

■ Meanwhile, for sauce, in a small skillet or saucepan cook garlic in hot oil till tender. In a small mixing bowl combine cornstarch, vinegar, and water. Carefully add to skillet. Cook and stir till sauce is slightly thickened and bubbly. Cook and stir for 1 minute more. Set aside.

■ To assemble lumpia, place a lumpia or spring roll wrapper on a flat surface in front of you. Spoon 2 tablespoons of the filling nearly across the width of the wrapper. Roll the wrapper once to cover the filling, then fold sides towards center. Moisten edges with water and continue to roll tightly.

■ In a large skillet heat 1 inch of cooking oil to 365°. Fry lumpia, a few at a time, for 2 to 3 minutes, or till golden brown. Drain on paper towels. Serve immediately with sauce. *Makes 6 side-dish or 12 appetizer servings*

Per serving: 190 calories, 12 g protein, 14 g carbohydrate, 10 g total fat (2 g saturated), 68 mg cholesterol, 372 mg sodium, 186 mg potassium

Preparation Time: 40 minutes
Cooking Time: 6 to 9 minutes

STEPS AT A GLANCE	Page
PREPARING SAUCE INGREDIENTS	16
PEELING SHRIMP	36
MAKING LUMPIA	95

STEPS FOR MAKING LUMPIA

STEP 1 FILLING

Prepare the filling and place in a bowl nearby. Spoon 2 tablespoons of the filling across the width of each dough wrapper. Leave a slight margin of space at either end.

STEP 2 ROLLING

Roll the wrapper once to cover the filling, then fold the sides toward the center. Moisten the edges with water and continue to roll tightly.

STEP 3 FRYING

Heat oil to proper temperature in a large skillet. Drop a few lumpia at a time into the hot fat with a wide metal spatula. Cook until golden brown, remove, and drain.

Mushroom-filled Ravioli

Preparation Time: 1 hour
Cooking Time: 20 minutes

STEPS AT A GLANCE	Page
MAKING PASTA	8–14
STUFFING PASTA	88
PREPARING SAUCE INGREDIENTS	16

Ravioli with a filling of thyme-scented mushrooms: elegant fare for any special occasion.

A mixture of several types of mushrooms will add a deep, woodsy flavor to the ravioli filling. These make a beautiful first course, light supper, or hot hors d'oeuvre. For the latter, serve the ravioli in a chafing dish with toothpicks for spearing.

■ Prepare spinach pasta as directed, except roll each portion of dough into an 8x12-inch rectangle. Cover and set aside.

■ For filling, in a large skillet cook mushrooms, onion, and garlic in hot margarine or butter for 5 minutes, or till tender. In a medium mixing bowl combine egg, bread crumbs, Parmesan cheese, and thyme. Stir in mushroom mixture. Set aside.

■ To make ravioli, cut each portion of pasta into four 2x12-inch strips. Brush one side of one strip with water. Place about 2 teaspoons of filling every 2 inches, beginning 1 inch from the end on one of the pieces. Take second strip and place it over the top of the filling. Press pasta together between the mounds of filling. Use a 2-inch ravioli cutter, square cookie cutter, or sharp knife to cut between the ravioli. Press the edges down firmly again to seal. Repeat with remaining pasta and filling.

■ For sauce, in a small saucepan heat whipping cream over medium heat for about 15 minutes, or till bubbly, stirring frequently. Boil gently for 3 to 4 minutes more.

■ Meanwhile, in a large saucepan or pasta pot bring 3 quarts water to boiling. Add half of the pasta. Reduce heat slightly. Boil, uncovered, for 6 to 8 minutes, or till al dente, stirring occasionally. Remove pasta from boiling water with a slotted spoon and place in a greased casserole. Cover and keep warm in a preheated 300° oven while cooking remaining pasta. Pour thickened cream over cooked ravioli. If desired, sprinkle with fresh thyme. Serve immediately.

Makes 6 side-dish servings

Per serving: 262 calories, 7 g protein, 16 g carbohydrate, 20 g total fat (11 g saturated), 111 mg cholesterol, 301 mg sodium, 164 mg potassium

96

INGREDIENTS

2	PORTIONS (8 OUNCES) SPINACH PASTA (PAGE 14)

FILLING

1-1/3	CUPS FINELY CHOPPED FRESH MUSHROOMS
1/3	CUP FINELY CHOPPED ONION
1	CLOVE GARLIC, MINCED
1	TABLESPOON MARGARINE *OR* BUTTER
1	BEATEN EGG
1/4	CUP SEASONED FINE DRY BREAD CRUMBS
1/4	CUP GRATED PARMESAN CHEESE
1/4	TEASPOON DRIED THYME, CRUSHED

SAUCE

1	CUP WHIPPING CREAM
	FRESH THYME LEAVES (OPTIONAL)

Meat-stuffed Ravioli

INGREDIENTS

Preparation Time: 1 hour
Cooking Time: 12 to 16 minutes

2	PORTIONS (8 OUNCES) HOMEMADE PASTA (PAGE 14)
	CLASSIC TOMATO SAUCE (PAGE 18) *OR* 3 1/2 CUPS SPAGHETTI SAUCE
1	BEATEN EGG
3/4	CUP SOFT BREAD CRUMBS (1 SLICE)
2	TABLESPOONS DRY RED WINE
1	CLOVE GARLIC, MINCED
1	TEASPOON FENNEL SEED, CRUSHED
1/4	TEASPOON ITALIAN SEASONING, CRUSHED
1/4	TEASPOON SALT
1/8	TEASPOON PEPPER
12	OUNCES LEAN GROUND BEEF *OR* VEAL
1/4	CUP GRATED PARMESAN CHEESE

97

*U*sing egg roll wrappers is a good way to cut down on the preparation time for this recipe. Simply substitute 48 wrappers for the pasta and cook for 6 to 8 minutes.

■ Prepare fresh pasta as directed, except roll each portion of the dough into an 8x12-inch rectangle. Cover and set aside.

■ If using classic tomato sauce, prepare as directed. Set aside.

■ In a large mixing bowl stir together egg, bread crumbs, wine, garlic, fennel seed, Italian seasoning, salt, and pepper. Add beef or veal and mix well. Shape meat mixture into a 6x4-inch rectangle. Using a long knife, cut into twenty-four 1-inch squares.

■ To make ravioli, cut each portion of pasta into four 2x12-inch strips. Brush one side of one strip with water. Place 1 meat square every 2 inches, beginning 1 inch from the end on one of the pieces. Take the second strip of pasta and place it over the top of the filling. Press pasta together between the meat squares. Use a 2-inch ravioli cutter, square cookie cutter, or sharp knife to cut between the ravioli. Press the edges down firmly again to seal. Repeat with remaining pasta and filling.

■ Meanwhile, in a large saucepan or pasta pot bring 3 quarts water to boiling. Add half of the ravioli. Reduce heat slightly. Boil, uncovered, for 6 to 8 minutes, or till meat in ravioli is no longer pink and pasta is al dente, stirring occasionally. Remove ravioli from boiling water with a slotted spoon and place in a greased casserole. Cover and keep warm in a preheated 300° oven while cooking remaining ravioli. Serve tomato sauce over hot cooked ravioli. Sprinkle with Parmesan cheese and serve immediately.

Makes 4 main-dish servings

Per serving: 642 calories, 33 g protein, 77 g carbohydrate, 24 g total fat (6 g saturated), 165 mg cholesterol, 638 mg sodium, 1,576 mg potassium

With very little effort, you can make ravioli that compare to the best restaurant pasta. Serve with a simple tomato sauce, a salad, and garlic bread.

Ham Tortellini with Cheese Sauce

Tiny stuffed tortellini are made from little circles of spinach pasta that are filled, sealed, and folded in half.

Preparation Time: 1½ hours
Cooking Time: 12 to 16 minutes

INGREDIENTS

2	PORTIONS (8 OUNCES) SPINACH PASTA (PAGE 14)

FILLING

2	TABLESPOONS FINELY CHOPPED CELERY
2	TABLESPOONS FINELY CHOPPED ONION
2	TEASPOONS MARGARINE OR BUTTER
4	OUNCES GROUND FULLY COOKED HAM
1	BEATEN EGG YOLK

SAUCE

2	TABLESPOONS MARGARINE OR BUTTER
4	TEASPOONS ALL-PURPOSE FLOUR
1	CUP MILK
1/2	CUP SHREDDED SWISS CHEESE
2	TABLESPOONS SNIPPED FRESH PARSLEY

98

*H*ere's an unusual pasta: our version of an old deli favorite, ham and Swiss. Using spinach pasta adds a nice color to the dish.

■ Prepare and roll spinach pasta as directed. With a 1½-inch-round cutter, cut 96 circles from dough. Cover and set aside.

■ For filling, cook celery and onion in hot margarine or butter till tender. Remove from heat and stir in ham and egg yolk. Place about ¼ teaspoon of the filling in the center of each circle. Fold circle in half and press edges together. Place your finger against the fold and bring corners together, pressing to seal. Let stand for 10 minutes. In a large saucepan or pasta pot bring 3 quarts water to boiling. Add half of the tortellini. Reduce heat slightly. Boil, uncovered, for 6 to 8 minutes, or till al dente, stirring occasionally. Remove pasta from boiling water with a slotted spoon and place in a greased casserole. Cover and keep warm in a preheated 300° oven while cooking remaining pasta.

■ Meanwhile, for sauce, in a small saucepan melt margarine or butter. Stir in flour. Add milk all at once. Cook and stir till thickened and bubbly. Cook and stir for 1 minute more. Stir in Swiss cheese and parsley till cheese is melted.

■ Spoon sauce over hot cooked tortellini and serve immediately.

Makes 4 main-dish servings

Per serving: 317 calories, 17 g protein, 24 g carbohydrate, 17 g total fat (6 g saturated), 115 mg cholesterol, 592 mg sodium, 316 mg potassium

Agnolotti Florentine with Mornay Sauce

*A*gnolotti *("fat little lambs") and ravioli are essentially the same dish, except that the former are shaped into half-moons while ravioli are square. Tomato or spinach pasta (page 14) complements the spinach filling and the creamy cheese sauce.*

■ For spinach agnolotti, prepare fresh pasta as directed, except roll each portion of the dough into an 8x12-inch rectangle. Cover and set aside. In a food processor bowl or blender container process or blend cooked spinach and 1 egg till nearly smooth. Transfer mixture to a medium mixing bowl and stir in cream cheese, prosciutto, Parmesan cheese, and nutmeg. Cover and refrigerate till needed.

■ Cut dough into circles with a 2-inch fluted cutter, place about ½ teaspoon of filling on each round, brush edge with water, then fold in half to create a half-moon shape. Repeat with remaining pasta and filling.

■ For Mornay sauce, in a small saucepan melt margarine or butter. Stir in flour. Add milk all at once. Cook and stir over medium heat till thickened and bubbly. Cook and stir for 1 minute more. Stir in fontina cheese till melted. Keep warm.

■ Meanwhile, in a large saucepan or pasta pot bring 3 quarts water to boiling. Add half of the pasta. Reduce heat slightly. Boil, uncovered, for 8 to 10 minutes, or till al dente, stirring occasionally. Remove pasta from boiling water with a slotted spoon and place in a greased casserole. Cover and keep warm in a preheated 300° oven while cooking remaining pasta. Spoon Mornay sauce over hot cooked pasta and serve at once.

Makes 6 side-dish servings

Per serving: 304 calories, 15 g protein, 18 g carbohydrate, 19 g total fat (7 g saturated), 140 mg cholesterol, 283 mg sodium, 199 mg potassium

Preparation Time: 1½ hours
Cooking Time: 16 to 20 minutes

INGREDIENTS

SPINACH AGNOLOTTI

4	PORTIONS (1 POUND) TOMATO *OR* SPINACH PASTA (PAGE 14)
5	CUPS FRESH SPINACH *OR* HALF OF A 10-OUNCE PACKAGE FROZEN CHOPPED SPINACH, COOKED AND WELL DRAINED
1	EGG YOLK
1	3-OUNCE PACKAGE CREAM CHEESE WITH CHIVES, SOFTENED
1/4	CUP FINELY CHOPPED PROSCIUTTO (1 OUNCE)
2	TABLESPOONS GRATED PARMESAN CHEESE
1/8	TEASPOON GROUND NUTMEG

MORNAY SAUCE

2	TABLESPOONS MARGARINE *OR* BUTTER
2	TABLESPOONS ALL-PURPOSE FLOUR
1-1/4	CUPS MILK
1	CUP SHREDDED FONTINA CHEESE (4 OUNCES)

99

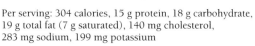

STEPS AT A GLANCE	Page
MAKING PASTA	8–14
GRATING NUTMEG	21
STUFFING PASTA	88

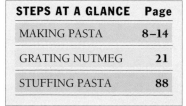

Rounds of pasta dough are stamped out with a scalloped cutter, filled with spinach, ham, and cheeses, then folded into charming half-moons.

Cheese Tortellini with Sausage & Peppers

Preparation Time: 45 minutes
Cooking Time: 20 minutes

INGREDIENTS

12	OUNCES FRESH SWEET ITALIAN SAUSAGE LINKS
1	CUP WATER
1	CUP CHOPPED ONION
2	CLOVES GARLIC, MINCED
2	TEASPOONS OLIVE OIL OR COOKING OIL
1	28-OUNCE CAN WHOLE ITALIAN-STYLE TOMATOES, CUT UP
1/4	CUP TOMATO PASTE
1/4	CUP DRY RED WINE
2	TABLESPOONS SNIPPED FRESH PARSLEY
1	TEASPOON DRIED OREGANO, CRUSHED
1/4	TEASPOON CRUSHED RED PEPPER
1	MEDIUM GREEN SWEET PEPPER, CUT INTO 1/2-INCH PIECES
12	OUNCES DRIED OR 16 OUNCES FRESH CHEESE-FILLED TORTELLINI OR RAVIOLI, OR SPINACH AGNOLOTTI (PAGE 99)

100

This sauce isn't shy: It is assertively seasoned with crushed red pepper, garlic, and wine. It cooks up deep red and spicy, a nice contrast to the mildness of the cheese-filled tortellini.

■ In a large skillet combine sausage links and water. Bring to boiling; reduce heat. Cover and simmer for 15 minutes, or till juices run clear. Drain off water. Cook sausage links, uncovered, for 2 to 4 minutes more, or till brown, turning frequently. Remove from skillet; cool. Bias-slice into ½-inch pieces. Wipe skillet clean with paper towels.

■ In the same skillet, cook onion and garlic in hot oil till tender but not brown. Stir in tomatoes, tomato paste, wine, parsley, oregano, and crushed red pepper. Add sausage and green sweet pepper to skillet. Bring to boiling; reduce heat. Cover and simmer for 20 minutes, or to desired consistency.

■ Meanwhile, in a large saucepan or pasta pot bring 3 quarts water to boiling. Add pasta. Reduce heat slightly. Boil, uncovered, 15 minutes for dried pasta or 8 to 10 minutes for fresh, or till al dente, stirring occasionally. (Or, cook according to package directions.) Immediately drain. Return pasta to warm saucepan. Pour sausage mixture over hot cooked pasta. Serve immediately.

Makes 4 to 5 main-dish servings

Per serving: 654 calories, 35 g protein, 73 g carbohydrate, 24 g total fat (6 g saturated), 111 mg cholesterol, 1,441 mg sodium, 946 mg potassium

Sausage and peppers, a very compatible duo, star in a highly seasoned tomato sauce for cheese tortellini.

Ravioli with Walnut Sauce

Grated fresh ginger, quickly sautéed with chopped onion and walnuts, adds a refreshing note to a quick pasta dish. Top with tangy crumbled blue cheese or feta cheese.

STEPS AT A GLANCE	Page
MAKING PASTA	8–14
STUFFING PASTA	88
CRUMBLING CHEESE	39

Preparation Time: 15 minutes
Cooking Time: 3 to 4 minutes

INGREDIENTS

9	OUNCES PURCHASED FRESH RAVIOLI *OR* HOMEMADE MUSH-ROOM-FILLED RAVIOLI (PAGE 96) *OR* MEAT- STUFFED RAVIOLI (PAGE 97)
1/4	CUP CHOPPED WALNUTS, PECANS, *OR* ALMONDS
4	GREEN ONIONS, THINLY SLICED
1	TEASPOON GRATED GINGERROOT
3	TABLESPOONS MARGARINE *OR* BUTTER
1/4	CUP CRUMBLED BLUE CHEESE, FETA CHEESE, *OR* GRATED PARMESAN CHEESE (OPTIONAL)

101

*U*sing store-bought fresh ravioli makes this a quick-and-easy meal to whip up after a busy day. If you prefer, serve the sauce over your own homemade ravioli (pages 96 and 97).

■ In a large saucepan or pasta pot bring 3 quarts water to boiling. Add pasta. Reduce heat slightly. Boil, uncovered, for 6 to 8 minutes, or till al dente, stirring occasionally. (Or, cook according to package directions.) Immediately drain.

■ Meanwhile, in a medium skillet cook and stir the nuts, onions, and ginger-root in hot margarine or butter for 3 to 4 minutes, or till onions are tender but not brown and nuts are lightly toasted. Pour nut mixture over hot cooked ravioli. If desired, sprinkle with blue cheese, feta cheese, or Parmesan cheese. Serve immediately.

Makes 4 main-dish servings

Per serving: 360 calories, 13 g protein, 21 g carbohydrate, 25 g total fat (4 g saturated), 59 mg cholesterol, 538 mg sodium, 79 mg potassium

Manicotti with Roasted Vegetables

*T*o make fresh manicotti shells, use two portions (about 8 ounces) of Homemade Pasta (page 14). Roll dough into a 14x10-inch rectangle about ⅛ inch thick. Cut the dough into eight 5x3½-inch rectangles. Cook for 2 to 3 minutes and continue as directed, following the directions for filling manicotti on page 91, step 4.

■ Cut the sweet peppers into bite-size strips. Cut the onion into small wedges. Bias-slice the yellow summer squash and zucchini into ¼-inch-thick pieces. In a 13x9x2-inch baking pan combine the sweet peppers, onion, yellow summer squash, zucchini, and garlic. Drizzle with olive oil or cooking oil. Bake in a preheated 425° oven for about 30 minutes, or till tender, stirring once or twice. Remove garlic cloves. Reduce oven temperature to 350°.

■ Meanwhile, if using classic tomato sauce, prepare as directed. Set aside. In a large saucepan or pasta pot bring 3 quarts water to boiling. Add manicotti shells. Reduce heat slightly. Boil, uncovered, about 18 minutes, or till al dente, stirring occasionally. (Or, cook according to package directions.) Immediately drain. Rinse with cold water and drain again.

■ In a medium mixing bowl stir together the eggs, mozzarella cheese, ricotta cheese, Parmesan cheese, chives, and pepper.

■ To fill manicotti shells, spoon about ⅓ cup of the cheese mixture into each one. Arrange manicotti in a 3-quart rectangular baking dish. Pour tomato sauce over the top. Arrange roasted vegetables on top of the sauce. Bake, covered, in the 350° oven for 35 to 40 minutes, or till heated through.

Makes 4 to 6 main-dish servings

Per serving: 720 calories, 41 g protein, 67 g carbohydrate, 34 g total fat (14 g saturated), 174 mg cholesterol, 885 mg sodium, 1,726 mg potassium

102

Preparation Time: 1 hour (includes sauce)
Baking Time: 65 to 75 minutes

INGREDIENTS

1/2	OF A MEDIUM GREEN SWEET PEPPER
1/2	OF A MEDIUM ORANGE *OR* RED SWEET PEPPER
1/2	OF A MEDIUM YELLOW SWEET PEPPER
1/2	OF A MEDIUM ONION
1	MEDIUM YELLOW SUMMER SQUASH
1	MEDIUM ZUCCHINI
2	CLOVES GARLIC, PEELED
1	TABLESPOON OLIVE OIL *OR* COOKING OIL
	CLASSIC TOMATO SAUCE (PAGE 18) *OR* 3-1/2 CUPS SPAGHETTI SAUCE
8	DRIED MANICOTTI SHELLS
2	BEATEN EGGS
2	CUPS SHREDDED MOZZARELLA CHEESE (8 OUNCES)
1-1/2	CUPS RICOTTA CHEESE
1/3	CUP GRATED PARMESAN CHEESE
2	TABLESPOONS SNIPPED FRESH CHIVES
1/4	TEASPOON GROUND WHITE *OR* BLACK PEPPER

Green peppers, summer squash, and tomatoes add the bright colors and sun-drenched flavors of an Italian kitchen garden to cheese-filled manicotti.

Broiled Spinach Cannelloni

Preparation Time: 1 hour
Broiling Time: 5 minutes

INGREDIENTS

CANNELLONI

1	PORTION (4 OUNCES) HOMEMADE PASTA (PAGE 14)
5	CUPS FRESH SPINACH OR 1/2 OF A 10-OUNCE PACKAGE FROZEN CHOPPED SPINACH, THAWED
3	OR 4 CLOVES GARLIC, PEELED AND QUARTERED
2	TABLESPOONS OLIVE OIL OR COOKING OIL
1/4	CUP GRATED PARMESAN CHEESE
2	TABLESPOONS FINE DRY BREAD CRUMBS
1/8	TEASPOON GROUND RED PEPPER
2	TEASPOONS OLIVE OIL OR COOKING OIL
1	TABLESPOON GRATED PARMESAN CHEESE

SAUCE

1/2	CUP CHICKEN BROTH
1-1/2	TEASPOONS CORNSTARCH
1	TEASPOON MARGARINE OR BUTTER
1	TABLESPOON LEMON JUICE
1	TABLESPOON WHIPPING CREAM
1/4	CUP TOASTED PINE NUTS

*T*o save time, use 6 dried lasagne noodles instead of making the fresh pasta. Cook the noodles according to package directions and drain. Cut each noodle into 3 pieces for 9 servings. Spoon the filling onto the pasta and continue as directed in the recipe.

■ For cannelloni, prepare and roll homemade pasta as directed. Cut into sixteen 3-inch-squares. Cover and set aside.

■ Trim and wash fresh spinach (if using); finely chop. In a large skillet cook and stir garlic in 2 tablespoons hot olive oil or cooking oil over medium-high heat for 30 seconds. Add fresh or thawed frozen spinach. Cook and stir for 1 to 2 minutes, or till fresh spinach is wilted or thawed spinach is heated through. Drain thoroughly in a colander, squeezing out excess liquid. In a medium mixing bowl combine spinach, ¼ cup Parmesan cheese, bread crumbs, and ground red pepper.

■ Meanwhile, in a large saucepan or pasta pot bring 3 quarts water to boiling. Add pasta. Reduce heat slightly. Boil, uncovered, for 3 to 4 minutes, or till al dente, stirring occasionally. Use a slotted spoon to carefully lift pasta out of water and into a colander. Rinse with cold water. Drain well. Carefully spread on a damp cloth towel.

■ To assemble, place 1 scant tablespoon filling along one end of each pasta square. Roll the dough tightly around the filling. Place on a greased baking sheet. Drizzle 2 teaspoons olive oil or cooking oil over pasta. Sprinkle with 1 tablespoon Parmesan cheese. Broil 6 inches from the heat for 5 minutes, or till golden brown.

■ Meanwhile, for sauce, in a small saucepan combine chicken broth and cornstarch; add margarine or butter. Cook and stir till thickened and bubbly. Stir in lemon juice and whipping cream and heat through. Spoon over cannelloni; sprinkle with toasted pine nuts.

Makes 8 side-dish servings

Per serving: 182 calories, 7 g protein, 20 g carbohydrate, 10 g total fat (2 g saturated), 10 mg cholesterol, 147 mg sodium, 261 mg potassium

103

Spinach-filled pasta tubes are placed under the broiler for a golden-brown finish, then served with a lemony cream sauce and pine nuts.

Classic Cannelloni

*B*oth the tomato sauce and chicken filling can be prepared a day ahead and refrigerated until you assemble the cannelloni. Let the sauce and filling sit at room temperature for about 15 minutes so they will bake in the specified time.

■ Prepare and roll homemade pasta as directed. Cut into sixteen 3-inch squares. Cover and set aside.

■ Prepare classic tomato sauce as directed. Set aside. For Parmesan sauce, in a small saucepan melt margarine or butter. Stir in flour, salt, and pepper. Add milk all at once. Cook and stir over medium heat till thickened and bubbly. Stir in Parmesan cheese and sour cream. Set aside.

■ For chicken filling, heat oil in a large skillet. Add chicken, onion, parsley, garlic, salt, and pepper. Cook for 5 minutes, or till chicken is tender and no longer pink and onion is tender. Cool slightly. Place chicken mixture and prosciutto or ham in a food processor bowl or blender container. Process or blend till mixture is finely chopped. Transfer filling to a medium mixing bowl and stir in ¾ cup of the Parmesan sauce.

■ In a large saucepan or pasta pot bring 3 quarts water to boiling. Add pasta. Reduce heat slightly. Boil, uncovered, for 3 to 4 minutes, or till al dente, stirring occasionally. Drain.

■ Place a scant 2 tablespoons of the chicken filling along one edge of each pasta square. Roll dough tightly around the filling. Place in a greased 3-quart rectangular baking dish. Pour remaining Parmesan sauce over half of the pasta. Pour tomato sauce over remaining pasta. Sprinkle with 1 tablespoon Parmesan cheese. Bake in a preheated 350° oven for 30 to 35 minutes, or till heated through. Serve immediately.

Makes 4 main-dish or 8 side-dish servings

Per serving: 490 calories, 27 g protein, 35 g carbohydrate, 28 g total fat (10 g saturated), 81 mg cholesterol, 1,066 mg sodium, 964 mg potassium

Preparation Time: 1½ hours
Baking Time: 30 to 35 minutes

INGREDIENTS

1	PORTION (4 OUNCES) HOMEMADE PASTA (PAGE 14)
1-1/2	CUPS CLASSIC TOMATO SAUCE (PAGE 18) *OR* SPAGHETTI SAUCE

PARMESAN SAUCE

1/4	CUP MARGARINE *OR* BUTTER
1/4	CUP ALL-PURPOSE FLOUR
1/4	TEASPOON SALT
1/8	TEASPOON PEPPER
1-1/2	CUPS MILK
1/3	CUP GRATED PARMESAN CHEESE
3	TABLESPOONS DAIRY SOUR CREAM

CHICKEN FILLING

1	TABLESPOON OLIVE OIL *OR* COOKING OIL
8	OUNCES BONELESS, SKINLESS CHICKEN BREAST HALVES, CHOPPED
1/2	CUP CHOPPED ONION
1/4	CUP SNIPPED FRESH PARSLEY
1	CLOVE GARLIC, MINCED
1/4	TEASPOON SALT
1/8	TEASPOON PEPPER
2	OUNCES SLICED PROSCIUTTO *OR* HAM, CHOPPED (1/2 CUP)
1	TABLESPOON GRATED PARMESAN CHEESE

Two sauces, one made with fresh tomatoes and herbs and the other a béchamel with Parmesan, top homemade cannelloni.

Pasta Salads

Steps for Making Pasta Salads

COLANDER

SERVING BOWL

SCREW-TOP JAR

SERVING FORK
AND SPOON

BASIC TOOLS FOR MAKING PASTA SALADS

Always drain pasta thoroughly in a colander or strainer before tossing with other ingredients in a wide, shallow bowl. A small glass jar with a lid is handy for blending and storing salad dressings.

NOT SURPRISINGLY, pasta has the same affinity for salad dressings as it does for other sauces. Bathed in herb-flavored emulsions of fruity olive oil and tart vinegar, or tossed with creamy yogurt or sour cream blends, pasta absorbs some of the dressing and releases wonderful flavor with each bite. The tender chewiness of pasta contributes substance and textural contrast to a salad and holds its own against other additions like ripe olives, crunchy bits of celery and sweet pepper, chunks of spicy salami, and toasted chopped nuts.

Pasta salads are delicious warm-weather companions to grilled meats, poultry, and fish. As a main course, they make appealing light lunches or suppers when accompanied with sliced fruit and a good, crusty loaf. They are simple to put together and can be assembled just far enough in advance to marry the flavors.

Pasta for salad should always be cooked just until al dente, never a second more. Nothing is worse than

pasta that is too soft or that falls apart when the salad is tossed together. Drain the pasta thoroughly as soon as it is done, then rinse to stop the cooking and prevent the pasta from sticking together. Give it a good shake in the colander to pull off any water that remains. If water clings to the pasta, the flavor of the dressing will be diluted, much as it is when mixed with salad greens that haven't been dried properly.

If the dressing calls for olive oil, use a good one. The best are extra-virgin oils, from the first pressing of the olive. These oils vary in their fruitiness and offer a spectrum of color that ranges from verdant green to a golden bronze. Purchase small amounts of several different kinds until you find one or two that please you. Experiment with vinegars as well. A wide variety are available to give your dressings excitement, from deep-toned, surprisingly sweet and mellow balsamic to red and white wine vinegars with delicate infusions of herbs or fruit.

drain away as much water as possible after rinsing so none remains to dilute the dressing

dressings with a mayonnaise base blend better when whisked in a bowl

STEP 1 RINSING PASTA

Cook the pasta in 3 quarts of rapidly boiling water until it is al dente. Immediately drain off the cooking water. Rinse under cold running water to separate the pasta; drain again thoroughly.

STEP 2 MAKING SALAD DRESSING

Place all ingredients in a glass jar with a lid. Secure the lid and shake vigorously until the ingredients are combined into an emulsion.

107

mix thoroughly, but with a light touch

STEP 3 TOSSING SALAD

Place all the salad ingredients in a wide, shallow serving bowl. Pour the dressing over the pasta mixture. With a large spoon and fork or two spoons, toss gently to coat all the ingredients with dressing.

Although this salad (page 116) specifies crinkled radiatori ("radiators"), you can substitute conchiglie ("shells") or any pasta of the same approximate size.

Curried Orzo Salad

Preparation Time: 25 minutes
Cooking Time: 5 to 8 minutes
Chilling Time: 2 to 24 hours

INGREDIENTS

1	CUP ORZO PASTA (6 OUNCES)
3/4	CUP CHOPPED PROSCIUTTO *OR* FULLY COOKED HAM
2	ORANGES, PEELED, SECTIONED, AND CUT INTO BITE-SIZE PIECES
1	CUP CHOPPED CELERY
1/3	CUP CHOPPED GREEN SWEET PEPPER
4	GREEN ONIONS, THINLY SLICED
1/3	CUP MAYONNAISE *OR* SALAD DRESSING
1/3	CUP PLAIN YOGURT
2	TABLESPOONS CHUTNEY, SNIPPED
3/4	TEASPOON CURRY POWDER
1	TO 2 TABLESPOONS MILK (OPTIONAL)
1/3	CUP PEANUTS

*H*ere we've used orzo, a barley-shaped pasta, in place of rice for a colorful and refreshing side salad with an Indian flavor. Other tiny pasta, such as rosamarina or riso, can also be used.

■ In a large saucepan or pasta pot bring 3 quarts water to boiling. Add pasta. Reduce heat slightly. Boil, uncovered, for 5 to 8 minutes, or till al dente, stirring occasionally. (Or, cook according to package directions.) Immediately drain. Rinse with cold water; drain again thoroughly.

■ In a large bowl combine cooked pasta, prosciutto or ham, oranges, celery, sweet pepper, and green onions.

■ In a small mixing bowl stir together mayonnaise or salad dressing, yogurt, chutney, and curry powder. Stir into pasta mixture. Cover and refrigerate for 2 to 24 hours.

■ Just before serving, if necessary, stir in milk to moisten salad. Sprinkle with peanuts before serving.

Makes 6 side-dish servings

Per serving: 328 calories, 11 g protein, 33 g carbohydrate, 18 g total fat (2 g saturated), 8 mg cholesterol, 384 mg sodium, 236 mg potassium

108

STEPS FOR SECTIONING AN ORANGE

STEP 1 CUTTING THE PEEL FROM AN ORANGE

Slice off the top and bottom of an orange with a sharp paring knife. Set one flat end on a cutting board. Hold the orange and, working top to bottom, cut off 1-inch-wide strips of peel.

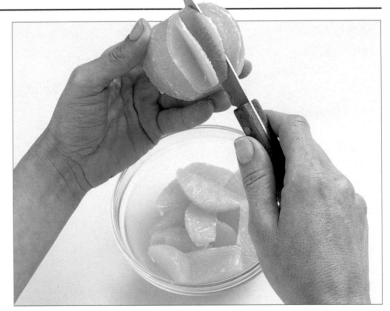

STEP 2 SECTIONING AN ORANGE

Work over a bowl to catch the juice. Insert a paring knife between the flesh and membrane of one section. Cut down to the center of the fruit. Turn the knife and slide it up the other side of the section to release it from the membrane on that side. Repeat with remaining sections.

Pair any grilled chicken or fish with this pasta salad that features the flavors of an Indian curry.

Big pasta shells filled with fresh vegetables are easily enjoyed out of hand. They are ideal buffet fare.

110

Eggplant Salad Shells

Make this earthy eggplant salad filling the night before so that all the flavors have a chance to meld. Serve as a hot-weather hors d'oeuvre, or as part of a cold buffet.

■ In a large skillet cook eggplant, onion, and celery in hot olive oil or cooking oil, covered, over medium heat for 5 to 8 minutes, or just till tender, stirring occasionally. Stir in undrained tomatoes, wine vinegar, tomato paste, sugar, salt, and red pepper. Cook, uncovered, over low heat for 5 minutes, or to desired consistency, stirring occasionally. Remove from heat. Stir in parsley and capers. Cool. Cover and refrigerate for 2 to 24 hours.

■ Let eggplant mixture stand at room temperature for 30 minutes. Stir in olives and pine nuts.

■ Meanwhile, in a large saucepan or pasta pot bring 3 quarts water to boiling. Add pasta. Reduce heat slightly. Boil, uncovered, for 23 to 25 minutes, or till al dente, stirring occasionally. (Or, cook according to package directions.) Immediately drain. Rinse with cold water; drain again thoroughly. Pat dry with paper towels.

■ To assemble, fill each shell with about ¼ cup of the eggplant mixture. Serve immediately.

Makes 6 side-dish or 18 appetizer servings

Per serving: 235 calories, 5 g protein, 28 g carbohydrate, 13 g total fat (2 g saturated), 0 mg cholesterol, 381 mg sodium, 472 mg potassium

INGREDIENTS

1	MEDIUM EGGPLANT, PEELED AND CUT INTO 1/2-INCH CUBES (ABOUT 4 CUPS)
3/4	CUP CHOPPED ONION
1/3	CUP CHOPPED CELERY
1/4	CUP OLIVE OIL *OR* COOKING OIL
1	14-1/2-OUNCE CAN DICED PEELED TOMATOES, UNDRAINED
3	TABLESPOONS RED WINE VINEGAR
2	TABLESPOONS TOMATO PASTE
1	TEASPOON SUGAR
1/2	TEASPOON SALT
	DASH GROUND RED PEPPER
1	TABLESPOON SNIPPED FRESH PARSLEY
1	TABLESPOON CAPERS, DRAINED
1/2	CUP SLICED PITTED RIPE OLIVES *OR* KALAMATA OLIVES, PITTED AND SLICED
2	TABLESPOONS TOASTED PINE NUTS *OR* CHOPPED ALMONDS
18	CONCHIGLIONI (LARGE PASTA SHELLS), ABOUT 4 OUNCES

111

STEP FOR STUFFING SHELLS

STEP 1 STUFFING SHELLS

Cup a cooked pasta shell in one hand and squeeze at both ends to open it. Scoop up some of the filling with a small spoon and insert into the shell. Repeat with the remaining shells and filling.

Hero Pasta Salad

Preparation Time: 20 minutes
Cooking Time: 8 to 12 minutes

INGREDIENTS

SALAD

3	OUNCES ROTINI, CAVATELLI, *OR* OTHER DRIED SHAPED PASTA (1 CUP)
1	CUP CUBED PROVOLONE CHEESE (4 OUNCES)
2	OUNCES FULLY COOKED HAM, CUT INTO THIN BITE-SIZE STRIPS (1/2 CUP)
2	OUNCES HARD SALAMI, CHOPPED (1/2 CUP)
1	SMALL RED ONION, HALVED THEN SLICED
1/2	CUP PEPPERONCINI, SLICED, *OR* SLICED MILD PEPPER RINGS
2	CUPS SHREDDED ICEBERG *OR* ROMAINE LETTUCE
1	LARGE TOMATO, COARSELY CHOPPED *OR* 1 CUP CHERRY TOMATOES, HALVED

DRESSING

3	TABLESPOONS OLIVE OIL *OR* SALAD OIL
3	TABLESPOONS BALSAMIC VINEGAR
1	TABLESPOON SNIPPED FRESH OREGANO *OR* 1/2 TEASPOON DRIED OREGANO, CRUSHED
2	SMALL CLOVES GARLIC, MINCED
1/4	TEASPOON DRY MUSTARD
1/8	TEASPOON COARSELY GROUND BLACK PEPPER

*T*his salad lends itself well to improvisation. Try adding some sliced imported olives, capers, chopped sweet peppers, or yellow or orange tomatoes. If making it ahead, wait to add the lettuce and tomato until just before serving time.

- In a large saucepan or pasta pot bring 3 quarts water to boiling. Add pasta. Reduce heat slightly. Boil, uncovered, for 8 to 12 minutes, or till pasta is al dente, stirring occasionally. (Or, cook according to package directions.) Immediately drain. Rinse with cold water and drain again thoroughly.

- In a large bowl toss together cooked pasta, provolone cheese, ham, salami, onion, and pepperoncini or pepper rings. Add lettuce and tomato; gently toss to mix.

- In a screw-top jar combine olive oil or salad oil, vinegar, oregano, garlic, dry mustard, and pepper. Cover; shake well. Pour over pasta mixture; toss to coat all ingredients with dressing and serve.

Makes 4 main-dish servings

Per serving: 426 calories, 20 g protein, 30 g carbohydrate, 25 g total fat (9 g saturated), 39 mg cholesterol, 1080 mg sodium, 449 mg potassium

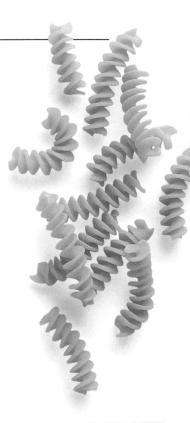

STEPS FOR SHREDDING LETTUCE AND SLICING ONION

STEP 1 SHREDDING LETTUCE

Hold one quarter of a head of iceberg lettuce firmly against a cutting board. Using a sharp knife, slice the lettuce thinly. The slices will separate into long, thin shreds.

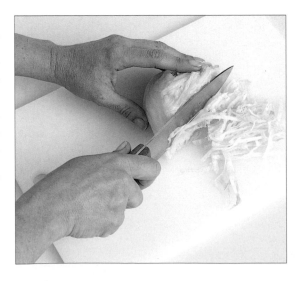

STEP 2 SLICING ONION

Peel the onion and cut in half lengthwise from top to root end. Place on a cutting board, cut-side down. Hold firmly and cut crosswise into 1/8-inch-thick slices. The slices will separate into half circles and then in pieces.

A mixed salad is always more interesting when the shapes, colors, and textures vary. Here rotini attractively contrasts with other ingredients cut into cubes, thin strips, and half-rounds.

Broiled Tuna & White Bean Salad

This is no ordinary tuna salad. It combines fresh tuna with cannellini beans, tomatoes, sweet yellow pepper, and penne pasta, all bathed in a lemon-and-herb dressing.

Preparation Time: 30 minutes
Broiling Time: 4 to 6 minutes
Cooking Time: 12 to 14 minutes

INGREDIENTS

12	OUNCES FRESH OR FROZEN TUNA STEAKS, 1/2 INCH THICK, OR TWO 6-1/2-OUNCE CANS SOLID WHITE TUNA, DRAINED AND BROKEN INTO CHUNKS
	OLIVE OIL OR SALAD OIL
8	OUNCES PENNE OR OTHER DRIED SHAPED PASTA
1/2	CUP OLIVE OIL OR SALAD OIL
1/4	CUP LEMON JUICE
1	19-OUNCE CAN CANNELLINI BEANS OR ONE 15-OUNCE CAN GREAT NORTHERN BEANS, DRAINED AND RINSED
2	MEDIUM TOMATOES, COARSELY CHOPPED
1/2	OF A MEDIUM YELLOW SWEET PEPPER, CUT INTO THIN BITE-SIZE STRIPS
2	SHALLOTS, FINELY CHOPPED
2	TABLESPOONS SNIPPED FRESH BASIL OR 1 TEASPOON DRIED BASIL, CRUSHED
1/4	TEASPOON SALT
1/8	TEASPOON PEPPER

114

*I*f you have leftovers, refrigerate them, but be sure to bring the salad back to room temperature before serving it again, or the dressing will be thick and lumpy.

- If using tuna steaks, thaw if frozen. Measure thickness of fish. Brush each side of tuna with oil. Broil tuna for 4 to 6 minutes per ½-inch thickness, or till tuna flakes easily when tested with a fork, turning once. Slice tuna diagonally into thin strips.

- In a large saucepan or pasta pot bring 3 quarts water to boiling. Add pasta. Reduce heat slightly. Boil, uncovered, for 12 to 14 minutes, or till al dente, stirring occasionally. (Or, cook according to package directions.) Immediately drain.

- In a large bowl combine cooked fresh or canned tuna, hot cooked pasta, beans, tomatoes, and sweet pepper.

- For dressing, in a screw-top jar combine ½ cup olive oil or salad oil, lemon juice, shallots, basil, salt, and pepper. Pour dressing over pasta mixture; toss gently and serve.

Makes 4 to 6 main-dish servings

Per serving: 519 calories, 16 g protein, 59 g carbohydrate, 28 g total fat (4 g saturated), 1 mg cholesterol, 369 mg sodium, 493 mg potassium

Warm Tomato–Feta Cheese Salad

Preparation Time: 50 minutes
Cooking Time: 10 to 12 minutes

INGREDIENTS

3	RIPE TOMATOES *OR* 6 RIPE PLUM TOMATOES, SEEDED AND CHOPPED
3	TABLESPOONS OLIVE OIL *OR* SALAD OIL
3	TABLESPOONS LEMON JUICE
1/4	CUP SNIPPED FRESH OREGANO *OR* 1 TEASPOON DRIED OREGANO, CRUSHED
2	CLOVES GARLIC, MINCED
1/8	TEASPOON PEPPER
1/3	CUP KALAMATA OLIVES, PITTED AND CHOPPED, *OR* PITTED RIPE OLIVES, CHOPPED
2	CUPS CRUMBLED FETA CHEESE (8 OUNCES)
8	OUNCES DRIED FARFALLE *OR* CONCHIGLIE, *OR* 16 OUNCES FRESH FARFALLE

*P*asta goes Greek. For a stronger and more authentic Greek flavor, use kalamata olives rather than pitted ripe olives. If you refrigerate any leftover salad, bring it to room temperature before serving.

■ Drain chopped tomatoes in a strainer for 15 minutes to remove excess liquid. In a large mixing bowl whisk the olive oil or salad oil into the lemon juice. Stir in oregano, garlic, and pepper. Add drained tomatoes, olives, and feta cheese. Toss to mix. Let mixture stand at room temperature for 30 minutes.

■ Meanwhile, in a large saucepan or pasta pot bring 3 quarts water to boiling. Add pasta. Reduce heat slightly. Boil, uncovered, for 10 to 12 minutes for dried pasta or 2 to 3 minutes for fresh, or till al dente, stirring occasionally. (Or, cook according to package directions.) Immediately drain. Return pasta to warm saucepan. Add tomato mixture to hot cooked pasta and toss to mix. Serve immediately.

Makes 8 to 10 side-dish servings

Per serving: 346 calories, 14 g protein, 29 g carbohydrate, 20 g total fat (10 g saturated), 57 mg cholesterol, 741 mg sodium, 187 mg potassium

115

Warm pasta tossed with marinated tomatoes, olives, and cheese makes a deeply flavorful salad.

Pasta Salad with Walnut Dressing

Preparation Time: 30 minutes
Cooking Time: 10 to 12 minutes

INGREDIENTS

8	OUNCES TRICOLORED *OR* PLAIN RADIATORI
1	CUP CHOPPED TOASTED WALNUTS
4	OUNCES CAPICOLLA *OR* FULLY COOKED HAM, CUT INTO SMALL CUBES (3/4 CUP)
1	CUP CRUMBLED BASIL-AND-TOMATO FETA CHEESE *OR* PLAIN FETA CHEESE (4 OUNCES)
1/2	CUP PITTED RIPE OLIVES *OR* UNSTUFFED GREEN OLIVES
1/4	CUP OLIVE OIL *OR* SALAD OIL
1/4	CUP LIME JUICE
1/4	CUP SNIPPED FRESH PARSLEY
1	CLOVE GARLIC, MINCED
1/4	TEASPOON SALT
1/8	TEASPOON PEPPER
	RED-TIPPED LEAF LETTUCE

*F*or the next potluck, volunteer to bring this easy and delicious salad. Combine the ingredients at home, but don't add the dressing until you get to the party. Carry the dressing in a jar, give it another shake, then pour over and toss.

■ In a large saucepan or pasta pot bring 3 quarts water to boiling. Add pasta. Reduce heat slightly. Boil, uncovered, for 10 to 12 minutes, or till al dente, stirring occasionally. (Or, cook according to package directions.) Immediately drain. Rinse with cold water; drain again thoroughly.

■ In a large bowl combine pasta, walnuts, capicolla or ham, feta cheese, and olives.

■ In a screw-top jar combine oil, lime juice, parsley, garlic, salt, and pepper. Cover and shake well. Pour over pasta mixture and gently toss to coat all ingredients with dressing. Serve salad on lettuce leaves.

Makes 4 main-dish servings

Per serving: 691 calories, 24 g protein, 55 g carbohydrate, 44 g total fat (9 g saturated), 42 mg cholesterol, 922 mg sodium, 425 mg potassium

STEPS AT A GLANCE	Page
COOKING PASTA	12
CRUMBLING CHEESE & TOASTING NUTS	39
MAKING PASTA SALADS	106

116

A dressing perfumed with tangy lime coats chunks of ham and cheese, olives, toasted walnuts, and multicolored pasta.

Tortellini-Mozzarella Salad

Little leaves of radicchio serve
as edible bowls for individual
portions of tortellini salad.

Preparation Time: 20 minutes
Cooking Time: 15 minutes

INGREDIENTS

5	OUNCES DRIED *OR* 10 OUNCES FRESH MEAT-FILLED TORTELLINI
1-1/2	CUPS CUBED PLAIN *OR* SMOKED MOZZARELLA (6 OUNCES)
1/2	OF A MEDIUM RED *OR* YELLOW SWEET PEPPER, CUBED
1/4	CUP SNIPPED FRESH BASIL *OR* 1 TEASPOON DRIED BASIL, CRUSHED
3	TABLESPOONS OLIVE OIL *OR* SALAD OIL
2	TABLESPOONS WHITE WINE VINEGAR
1	TABLESPOON BALSAMIC VINEGAR
1	SMALL HEAD RADICCHIO, DIVIDED INTO LEAF CUPS, *OR* 4 LEAF LETTUCE LEAVES

117

*I*f you need to make the salad ahead of time,
reserve the mozzarella and add it right before
serving time so it doesn't become mushy or rubbery.

■ In a large saucepan or pasta pot bring 3 quarts water to boiling. Add pasta. Reduce
heat slightly. Boil, uncovered, 15 minutes for dried pasta and 8 to 10 minutes for fresh,
or till al dente, stirring occasionally. (Or, cook according to package directions.)
Immediately drain. Rinse with cold water; drain again thoroughly.

■ In a medium mixing bowl combine cooked tortellini, mozzarella cheese, and red or
yellow sweet pepper.

■ In a screw-top jar combine basil, oil, white wine vinegar, and balsamic vinegar. Cover;
shake well. Pour over pasta mixture and gently toss to coat all ingredients with dressing. Serve salad in radicchio cups or on lettuce leaves.

Makes 4 main-dish servings

Per serving: 320 calories, 15 g protein, 21 g carbohydrate, 19 g total fat (8 g saturated), 46 mg cholesterol, 381 mg
sodium, 206 mg potassium

STEPS AT A GLANCE	Page
COOKING PASTA	12
MAKING PASTA SALADS	106

ARTICHOKES

ASPARAGUS

BASIL

BROCCOLI

CAPERS

CARROTS

CHEESES

CHIVES

FENNEL

CANNELLINI BEANS

GLOSSARY

The following glossary provides information on selecting, purchasing, and storing ingredients used in this book. Groups of ingredients are arranged clockwise from the upper left and are described in the text accordingly.

ARTICHOKES Only the fleshy base of the leaves and the meaty bottom of this edible bud of a tall, thistlelike plant are eaten; the rest of the leaf and the fuzzy interior choke are discarded. Artichokes are sold fresh year-round in sizes ranging from very small to very large; they are also available frozen, canned, and marinated. Select compact, heavy globes with tightly closed leaves; refrigerate in a plastic bag for up to 4 days.

ASPARAGUS This tender stalk with a tightly closed bud is prized for its delicate flavor and subtle hue (white asparagus, a delicacy, is not common). Crisp, straight, firm stalks with a tight cap are best. Wrap in damp paper towels and refrigerate in a plastic bag for up to 4 days.

BASIL With its affinity for sauces and tomato-based dishes, it isn't surprising to find basil in many pasta recipes. Intensely aromatic, fresh basil arrives in summer, when tomatoes are at their peak; dried basil may be found on the spice shelf all year. Store freshly cut stems in a little water, cover with plastic, and refrigerate for up to 2 days.

BROCCOLI Both the rigid green stalks and the tightly packed dark green or purplish-green heads (also called flowerets) are edible. Choose firm stalks and closed heads with deep color and no yellow areas. Refrigerate in a plastic bag for up to 4 days.

CANNELLINI BEANS Also known as white kidney beans, these are mild-flavored and meaty when cooked. They are available dried or canned. You may substitute great northern beans for dried cannellini.

CAPERS The pickled flower buds of a Mediterranean bush, capers add a piquant note to foods. Most markets stock them in jars with other condiments. Store opened jars in the refrigerator. Before using, drain off their vinegar brine.

CARROTS Choose firm, bright orange carrots; avoid those that are droopy or have cracks or dry spots. Refrigerate in a plastic bag, tops removed, for up to 2 weeks. Either peel or scrub before using. Tiny baby carrots are actually a separate variety prized for their delicate flavor and charming appearance. Store them as you would large carrots.

CHEESES The following cheeses often appear in pasta dishes: *Mascarpone* is rich and buttery, a cross between cream cheese and sour cream. Pliable, stringy *mozzarella* is used in baked dishes and salads. *Parmesan* is a hard and crumbly grating cheese with a nutty flavor; it is used as the finishing touch on most pasta dishes. Moist *ricotta* is mild and semi-sweet, with a soft, creamy texture. *Romano* is similar to Parmesan, but is sharper in taste. Storage length varies with the type of cheese, but all cheeses must be wrapped well and refrigerated to stay fresh.

CHIVES The long, hollow green leaves of this herb add bright color and a mild onion flavor to many dishes when snipped into little pieces. Fresh chives should not be wilted or damaged. Refrigerate, wrapped in damp paper towels and then in a plastic bag, for 3 to 4 days.

FENNEL With its tubular stalks and feathery leaves, this bulbous, creamy-white to pale-green vegetable resembles celery, but its flavor hints of licorice. Fresh fennel is delicious raw or cooked, while dried fennel seed is used as a seasoning. Select bulbs that are free of cracks or brown spots. Refrigerate in a plastic bag for up to 4 days.

GARLIC A bulb with a papery outer skin, a head of garlic is composed of numerous small cloves. Garlic may be used as a savory seasoning for almost every course of a meal. It is aromatic and almost bitter when raw, but becomes delicate and sweet when cooked. Fresh garlic should be plump and firm. Store whole bulbs in a cool, dark, dry place.

GINGERROOT The rhizome, or underground stem, of a semitropical plant, fresh gingerroot is a pungent seasoning with a lively, hot flavor and peppery aroma. Select stems that are firm and heavy, never shriveled, with taut, glossy skin. Wrap in a paper towel and refrigerate for up to 2 days. For longer storage, wrap airtight and freeze the unpeeled root.

KALE A member of the cabbage family, kale has ruffled dark green leaves and tastes like its cabbage relatives. It is eaten fresh or cooked, or used as a decorative garnish. Wash the leaves in cold water, dry, then refrigerate in a paper towel–lined plastic bag for up to 3 days.

OLIVE OIL A staple of Mediterranean cooking, olive oil imparts a clean, fruity flavor and golden-to-green color to salad dressings, grilled bread, and pasta sauces. Use extra-virgin oils, from the first pressing, for cold dishes. For sauces, use milder oils that can stand up to heat. Store in a dark spot away from heat for 6 months, or in the refrigerator for a year. (Chilled oil may get thick and cloudy; let it warm to room temperature before using.)

OREGANO Packed with robust flavor and aroma, oregano is a favorite herb of Italian and Greek cooks. Select bright green fresh oregano with firm stems. Look for dried whole or ground oregano with other spices. Refrigerate fresh oregano in a plastic bag for up to 3 days.

PANCETTA Unlike regular bacon, mild, spicy-sweet Italian pancetta is rarely smoked, although it is usually seasoned with pepper. It is sold in specialty markets in a roll rather than in a flat slab. Refrigerate it, well wrapped, for several weeks.

PARSLEY Widely used for cooking and garnish, parsley has such a clean, refreshing flavor that it is sometimes enjoyed as an after-meal digestive. Curly-leaf parsley is mild, while Italian parsley is flat-leafed and more pungent. Select healthy, lively looking bunches. To store, rinse and shake dry, wrap in paper towels and a plastic bag, and refrigerate for up to 1 week.

PROSCIUTTO This spicy, air-dried Italian ham is either eaten raw in paper-thin slices or heated as part of a recipe. Top-quality *prosciutto di Parma* is imported from Italy, but many excellent domestic varieties are available. Any Italian delicatessen and most specialty markets will stock both types. Wrap and refrigerate it for several weeks.

SQUASH Soft-skinned, slender green and yellow zucchini, straight and crookneck squashes, and pattypan squashes are classified as "summer" vegetables, although many are sold all year. Choose heavy, well-shaped squash without cracks or bruises. They will keep for up to 4 days in the refrigerator.

TOMATOES Botanically a fruit, tomatoes are eaten as a vegetable. Oval-shaped plum tomatoes (also called Italian or Roma) are thick and meaty, with less juice and smaller seeds than other varieties, which makes them ideal for sauces. They are sold fresh, or in cans sometimes flavored with basil and other seasonings. Other market forms include stewed tomatoes, cooked with celery, onions, and seasonings; tomato paste, a highly concentrated purée; and sweet, chewy dried tomatoes, either plain or oil-packed.

GARLIC

GINGERROOT

KALE

OLIVE OIL

OREGANO

PANCETTA

PARSLEY

PROSCIUTTO

SQUASH

TOMATOES

119

INDEX

USING THE NUTRITION ANALYSIS

Keep track of your daily nutrition needs by using the information we provide at the end of each recipe. We've analyzed the nutritional content of each recipe serving for you. When a recipe gives an ingredient substitution, we used the first choice in the analysis. If it makes a range of servings (such as 4 to 6), we used the smaller number. Ingredients listed as optional weren't included in the calculations.